Morgan

BODHI IN THE BRAIN

Yinnergy Meditation:
A Technological Path
to Enlightenment

Homages for Yinnergy

"Yinnergy is speeding up my path to awakening. Living in the era of capitalism, time is a valuable asset. In the midst of all the distractions, I can plug my headphones in, sit in a room then quiet my mind. Yinnergy is a strong introduction for beginners of meditation and people who have never practiced a traditional meditation technique."

- MORENO ZULU, Hip Hop Artist

"As a mentee, I have heard nearly a decade's worth of stories from Morgan regarding the power of mindfulness, well-being, and connecting with one's own sense of spirituality. Meditation, as a mindfulness practice, was something I had already been familiar with. However, Morgan was the first person to introduce me to the healing properties of sound technology. Personally, I struggle with my feelings quite often and at times I feel like they override my brain. Yinnergy gives the circuits of my heart and mind a break from being in override."

- FADUMA MOHAMED, Founder of OughtTheBox, Spoken Word Artist, Activist, Winner of the 2020 Emerging Artist Award

"Yinnergy is a profound technology that's simple in its method but powerful in its effects. I am quickly noticing its many benefits in my life, and it is has become one of my favourite methods to accelerate my spiritual growth. It is allowing me to purge what has been trapped in my subconscious that no longer serves me, expanding my awareness and igniting my creativity, deepening my connection to self and others, and enriching my life experience. It is a practice I deeply look forward to that supports me in catalyzing my highest expression of self."

- NATHALIE DELORME, Conscious Evolution Guide and Transformational Storyteller

"My day-to-day practices with Yinnergy have helped me deal with mental problems that have been holding me back, and heal from the pain they were causing. I always had trouble sleeping before and Yinnergy helped me sleep better. I'd also say that it's the reason for my creativity as it allowed me to learn how to accept and express myself. I feel more connected with myself spiritually, and it allows me to feel joyful and more at peace."

- JOEL S, Video Game Developer

"As a meditation instructor, it's easy for me to rely on my own practice without the help of a guide or sound. But when Morgan introduced me to Yinnergy, it really resonated with my spirit. Yinnergy is a beautiful remedy for anyone who needs healing and more calmness in their lives. It's soothing yet stimulating and deeply felt."

- PATRICIA MCPHERSON, Nidra Yoga Instructor

"Yinnergy has had a massively transformative impact on my life. When I was first exposed to it, I was just beginning to dive deeper into spirituality and self-awareness. During my first use, I found myself completely self-aware. It seemed as if, for the first time, I was fully connecting to every part of my being. It felt like my brain was being massaged and, as that happened, I could feel the depths of my brain's connection to my fingers, toes, organs, and other parts of my physical body. I also felt my mind's connection to another part of me that I could not fully explain because it was deeper than my physical body… It felt like an endless space that I can now only describe as my soul. Through Yinnergy I have been able to explore the depths of my mind, thoughts, body, and soul on a level that was very difficult to get to before. I cannot put into words what this program truly does for me, but I've been practicing with it for years. While using it, I feel a lot more grounded, focused, connected, creative, and my intuition increases tremendously. Whenever I have stopped using it for a long period (usually due to a lack of discipline) I really feel the difference, and I quickly find myself back on track. It's like a mind, body, and soul fitness routine. When you miss workouts, you notice the lack of results throughout your entire being. I personally enjoy seeing myself at my full potential, and Yinnergy is a massive asset in manifesting that experience."

- DYNESTI WILLIAMS, 2023 Winner of the R.I.S.E Community Initiative Awards

"Yinnergy is life changing. It heightened my experience and gave my mind something to focus on that wasn't my thoughts. Just sit, relax, be open, and observe. What a powerful metaphor. It awakened me to a new way of being, feeling, and viewing the world around me. I was able to see beauty, patterns and have moments of pure euphoria. When anyone is trying to get into meditation or struggling I always refer them to try this method out."

- EPIPHANY OZ, EVLOVE INC

"Yinnergy came into my life after my spiritual awakening, and it's one of the things I've been most grateful for. It has helped me to stretch out the moment between stimulus and response and become more deliberate with my choices. Because of that, "bad" news doesn't impact so much anymore. I also believe it has taken my poetry to another level, by helping me tap into what feels like a higher frequency. I've noticed that since practicing Yinnergy regularly, my poetic expression often incorporates the theme of transcendence, allowing me to speak about (and view life from) higher states of consciousness. On days when I feel overwhelmed, my spirit clearly tells me what I need to reach for to become centered: Yinnergy Meditation. Thank you Morgan O. Smith for bringing this gift into my life!"

- JUNGLE FLOWER, Poet, Photographer, Artist, TEDxRouge River Performer, Winner of the 2021 Mayor's Community Safety Award

"What can I say about Yinnergy...except that it works. I used to suffer from insomnia before I started practicing with Yinnergy. I would listen to the audio tracks every night before going to sleep, and by the time I was done listening, I would be asleep. The wonderful thing about Yinnergy was that it felt like food for the soul; it would resonate with my vibrational energy as if I was tapping into a higher source of energy. I would always feel illuminated with every session."

- MAMBU MASSAQUOI

It is important to be aware that the information provided in this book is intended to be used as guidance only. The treatments, strategies, and methods explained should be utilized to support, not replace, professional medical care or treatment. It is recommended to seek advice from a certified health care professional before attempting to treat any serious medical condition.

ISBN: 9781738879014 (paperback) / ISBN: 9781738879007 (e-book)

Copyright © 2023 Morgan O. Smith

All rights reserved. Published by Yinnergy Technologies and KeMor Centre for Innovative Development. Morgan O. Smith is the registered proprietor of Yinnergy Technologies, and Keda Edwards Pierre and Smith are the registered owners of KeMor Centre for Innovative Development.

https://true2soul.com/yinnergy

No part of this book may be used or reproduced in any manner without written permission from the author and publisher.

Names: Smith, Morgan O., author.

Title: Bodhi in the brain: Yinnergy meditation: a technological path to enlightenment / Morgan O. Smith

Subjects: BISAC: BODY, MIND & SPIRIT / Mindfulness & Meditation. | PHILOSOPHY / Mind & Body. | SELF-HELP / Spiritual.

Description: Unlock your full potential with Yinnergy Meditation. In this comprehensive guide, learn about the cutting-edge technology behind Yinnergy, its benefits on the brain, nervous system, and consciousness, and how it can change your life for the better. Discover the history of brainwave entrainment, the power of low carrier frequencies, and the role of different brainwaves. Explore the impact of Yinnergy on emotional and mental health, higher awareness, creativity, and spiritual enlightenment. Join the growing community of individuals who have transformed their lives with Yinnergy.

Cover Designer: nskvsky
Illustrator: Darnel Smith
Photographer: tonyxtones

I would like to give special thanks to Marko Rodin, Randy Powell, Ken Wilber, Arian Herbert, and the late Bill Harris, as well as my business partner Keda Edwards Pierre, my editor Nathalie Delorme, my children, my friends, and all my participants and clients who have put their trust in me with this technology.

Contents

Foreword 1

Introduction 5
    What is Bodhi? 6
    My Story 6

The Elements of Yinnergy 9
    The Split-Brain Theory 9
    The Process of Entrainment 10
    The History of Brainwave Technology 13
    Brainwaves: The Rhythms of the Brain 13

The Yinnergy Program 23
    The Benefits of Yinnergy 25
    Yinnergy and PTSD 27
    Yinnergy-Based Programs Within
    the School System 28
    Yinnergy-Based Programs
    Within the Prison System 29

The Technologies Behind Yinnergy 31
    Binaural Beats and Beat Frequencies 31
    Sine Tones and Sine Waves 33
    Pitch Frequencies and
    Carrier Frequencies 35

> Delta Brainwaves and
> the Subconscious 37

Vortex-Based Mathematics and Universal Patterns 41

> The Mathematical Basis
> of Yinnergy's Algorithm 41

Levels of Yinnergy 45

> The Sub-Categories of the Yinnergy Level 46
>
> Other Versions of Yinnergy 49

Yinnergy and Meditative Cross-Training 55

>> Traditional Meditation 55
>>
>> Self-Enquiry and Contemplation 56
>>
>> Christian Contemplative Prayer 57
>>
>> Neuro-Feedback Training 58
>>
>> Psychotherapy 58
>>
>> Breathwork 59
>>
>> Shadow Work ....
>>
>> 60

Yinnergy and Physical Health 63

> The Importance of Mindful Eating 64
>
> The Top 7 Nootropics 69
>
> Physical Activity 71

Yinnergy and Emotional Health 77

Yinnergy and Mental Health 81

Yinnergy and Spiritual Health 81

    The Fourth State of Consciousness 82

    The Fifth State of Consciousness 83

    The Seven Bodies of Manifestation 84

    Kundalini, Chakras, and the Nadis 91

    The Nadis 98

Yinnergy and the Thinking Mind 99

    The Multiple Intelligences Theory 99

    The Philosophy of Thinking 106

Yinnergy and Creativity 113

    The Power of Creativity 113

    Innovation 114

    Flow States 115

Yinnergy and Brain Health 117

    The Brain and its Function 117

    Facets of the Brain 118

    Neurons, Dendrites, and Synapses 123

    Microtubules 127

    Neural Melanin 133

    Brain Receptors 134

    The Olivary Nucleus 136

    Low Carrier Frequencies for Evolution 137

    Neurotransmitters and Hormones 144

    Nutrition for Brain and Gut Health 149

    The Gut 151

    Biohacking 155

    Brain Hacking 156

    Flow States and Being in the Zone 158

    Willpower and Self-Regulation 160

Yinnergy and Consciousness 163

    The Psyche and the Unconscious................... 163

Theory Maps for the Evolutionary Mind 169

    The Critical Brain Hypothesis 169

    Hierarchy of Needs... 178

    The 10,000 Hours Theory 180

    Open and Closed Systems............................. 182

    Chaos Theory 183

    The Evolutionary Process.............................. 185

    The One Hundredth Monkey Effect 186

    Integral Theory 187

    The Four Quadrants Model........................... 193

Western Technology Meets Eastern Traditions 197

    Mahayana Buddhism..................................... 197

    Zen 198

    Advaita Vedanta 198

    Vishishtadvaita Vedanta................................199

    Kashmir Shaivism 199

    Taoism... 200

Sikhism 200
Jainism 201

Yinnergy and the Healing Process 203
The Journey to Healing 203
The Self 208
The Evolution and Adaptation of the Self......... 215

Conclusion 219

Appendix 221
How Does Yinnergy Work?........................... 221
What is on the Yinnergy Soundtracks? 222
How Long Does It Take to
Complete the Pre-Level of Yinnergy? 223
What Are People Saying About Yinnergy? 223
Do You Have to Be an Experienced
Meditator to Use Yinnergy? 223
Instructions for Yinnergy Purge.................. 226

Vortex-Based Mathematics Bonus Chapter 229
Polarity 230
The Physics Behind Low Carrier Frequencies............ 232
The Importance of Sound
Physics in Brainwave Entrainment 234
An Example of the Yinnergy
Mathematical Equations 236
Panning 240

About the Author 245

Foreword

There we stood, staring at each other across a crowded room at the end of a community meeting — me, with a welcoming grin on my face, and him, returning with a solemn stare. I realized that my usually winning smile was failing miserably, and I wondered who this stoic man was, so still and contemplative in a room full of contentious discussions, frenetic energies, and battling agendas. Nonplussed, I made my way towards him from across the community room, determined to engage him in conversation. To his credit, he neither looked nor moved away as I approached, which he could have done quickly. Once I reached him, we didn't waste time on small talk or useless banter. Instead, we introduced ourselves, exchanged contact information and went on our way. Little did we know that day, with that brief conversation, began a friendship, professional relationship, and spiritual journey that has now spanned almost two decades. So started my connection to Morgan O. Smith.

What followed were years of hours-long discussions about spirituality, meditation, sacred mathematics, technology — and Yinnergy. It didn't matter what time of day, when the inclination hit; we'd talk mid-morning, mid-day, mid-night since time always became a non-issue once we engaged. I had no idea I was witnessing the birth of Yinnergy. In the interim, Morgan and I continued collaborating on numerous projects and programs for personal and spiritual development for youth and adults in communities, schools, and detention centres. Though I greatly respected and admired Morgan by this time and secretly viewed him as a polymathematician, I didn't understand brainwave entrainment back then. Then Morgan gave me a Yinnergy CD.

At this point, I should mention that the community gathering where I met Morgan was a police-community meeting, and I was also a police officer. With that said, I wasn't confident I could engage with Yinnergy without disrupting my capacity to do my job. Therefore, I held onto my CD for years, telling myself I would listen to it soon. I held off trying Yinnergy until one day, while on vacation, I decided to give it a try.

The effects were swift. My sleep improved, and this sound technology helped me deepen my practice of equanimity and transcendence. Though my spiritual awakening preceded my introduction to Yinnergy, I saw clearly how this sound technology buoyed, supported, deepened, and expanded my journey — personally, professionally and spiritually. As Yinnergy's binaural beat technology proved to be a powerful and transformative tool, I began to include it in my multi-modal practice.

Now retired from a 27-year career in policing, I'm an Ordained Minister, Reiki Master, Meditation Guide, Life Coach, and Founder of True2Soul Network — an organization devoted to safe and inclusive space for transformative healing, growth, and development. I encounter many people in search of healing, self-development, and growth. Yet, in my multi-modal practice, only a few modalities stand as powerfully as Yinnergy Meditation. I see this sound technology as an effective, non-invasive modality for mindfulness, spiritual connection, and personal growth — for myself, my clients, family and friends, including my husband, who is now also good friends with Morgan.

I mainly focus on resiliency development and trauma recovery in my practice. Several years ago, I ran a trauma-informed retreat for holistic therapists and practitioners. I included Yinnergy and Morgan in the program, and to this day, these practitioner participants remain connected, supportive, and on powerful journeys of transformation. We have seen such success in bringing together True2Soul's innovative programming with the powerful sound technology of Yinnergy Meditation that we've created the KeMor Centre for Innovative Development, with online programs devoted to personal growth, spiritual development, and life transformation.

I've come to see Morgan as an extraordinary human being, who walks his talk, allows himself to explore his intimate spiritual journey out loud and shares his life learnings to help others on their spiritual paths and growth journeys. I greatly admire this man, who doesn't speak outside of his own lived experiences and is passionately devoted to exploring enlightenment and eternally curious about the adventure — without apology or pretense.

I am beyond honoured to write this foreword. Bodhi in the Brain is more than a book. These writings form a guide to a spiritual journey and transformative healing experience, written by a man who is lovingly, generously, and passionately exposing the width and breadth of his journey to further that of others. It's taken me almost twenty years, but I finally realized that while Morgan may not have been smiling in that community room, his radiant spirit is what beckoned me forward.

Keda Edwards Pierre
Founder of True2Soul Network
Co-Founder of KeMor Centre for Innovative Development

Introduction

Welcome to Yinnergy Meditation: a new and innovative way to help you enhance your life based on the latest research in neuroscience and psychology. Easy-to-use and suitable for people of all ages, backgrounds, and levels of experience, this program works with your subconscious mind to help you overcome any negative patterns of thinking and behavior. It is based on the principles of neuroplasticity to improve your mental and emotional health, and train your brain to be more resilient and adaptable to stress. It has also been proven to be an effective tool to treat anxiety, depression, and other mental disorders.

Through a powerful and unique audio technology, Yinnergy Meditation will help you improve your overall well-being, reach a state of harmony and balance, and achieve higher levels of consciousness to tap into your innermost potential and create a life that is more fulfilling and satisfying.

What is Bodhi?

Put simply, Bodhi (Sanskrit for "enlightenment") refers in the Buddhist tradition to the experience of awakening or enlightenment that is achieved through the practice of meditation. Said to be liberating and transformative, it is a state of complete freedom from suffering, and from the cycle of birth and death, in which one is said to be in absolute harmony with the Universe, yet as the Universe.

There are many ways to achieve Bodhi, but one of the methods I can personally vouch for is with Yinnergy Meditation. The Yinnergy audio technology produces different brainwave frequencies that help induce a state of meditation, which can eventually lead to the ultimate event one may call Bodhi.

My Story

My name is Morgan and I am the creator of Yinnergy Meditation. I started meditating with brainwave entrainment back in 2002 after attending a series of hypnotherapy sessions, where I was introduced to light and sound machines, and loved how they made me feel. I eventually found a brainwave program online, and the results of my practice with it blew my mind. Everything started to change for me. Within that same year I got married, bought a home, and experienced bliss, lucid dreams, and natural highs and intoxications. I eventually left my career in the comedy and television industry, took some time off, and then decided to work within the not-for-profit sector with marginalized youth and families. Around that time, I started playing with sound generator software and read books on sound physics; I already had some training in musical engineering thanks to a course I took at Humber College years prior. I continued to meditate with the brainwave program every single day. Then in 2008, five years after I started working with it, I experienced my first spiritual awakening which changed the course of my life.

In 2010, after studying the work of mathematician Marko Rodin, I created Yinnergy Meditation which led to a series of profound awakenings and peak experiences. Many of my clients have used Yinnergy with extraordinary results in the areas of transpersonal experiences and personal development, career choices, self-expression, talent and skill improvement, and interpersonal and intrapersonal development. I have also created programs around this technology for use within the school system, both for students and teachers, and within detention centers for inmates. As I continued on my spiritual path for over 16 years and counting, I finally reached a full-blown non-dual awakening in December 2019 and experienced, with unwavering knowing, that everything within the universe is of one divine substance with no separation whatsoever.

This is only a tiny fraction of my personal story, but the immense depth of my journey has to do with the thousands of hours spent meditating with brainwave entrainment, which is why I would like to share this technology with you. So, if you are looking for a way to improve your well-being in many ways, create lasting changes in your life, and advance your spiritual transformation, the Yinnergy Meditation is a powerful tool that can support that.

The Elements of Yinnergy

The Split-Brain Theory

While developing Yinnergy and meditating with it throughout the years, I have been inspired by many extraordinary individuals who have contributed their time and energy to the various fields of knowledge that compose Yinnergy. One individual that comes to mind is neuropsychologist, Roger Wolcott Sperry. In the early 1960s, Sperry began conducting ground-breaking research on split-brain theory, which posits that the brain has two separate minds, with each side responsible for different functions. Sperry's work helped to revolutionize our understanding of the brain and its functions, and has had a major impact on the field of neuroscience.

This research contributed to one of the primary ideas behind the Yinnergy technology known as brain entrainment. If the two hemispheres of the brain are like two separate minds, each with its own thoughts, feelings, and experiences, then could it be that when the two hemispheres are stimulated by low carrier binaural beats using Yinnergy, that the two halves become more in sync with each other, resulting in a more cohesive and unified mind? Then, at this point, instead of the hemispheres lacking in communication, there would only be one shared language between both, and that is the internal universal language of the whole-integrated-self. Yinnergy is a binaural beat technology that uses different sound frequencies to encourage synchronization between the left and right hemispheres of the brain. This synchronization creates a state of whole-brain thinking (or whole-brain functioning), where one starts to think in stereo or use "surround thinking", so to speak.

The Process of Entrainment

Entrainment is a phenomenon that occurs when two or more oscillating bodies influence each other, resulting in their oscillations becoming synchronized. It is a process of two or more periodicities (events occurring in regularly spaced intervals of time) matching or attuning to each other. The word entrainment comes from the French term "entrainer", which means "to train" or "to lead".

Entrainment occurs in nature when two objects with different natural frequencies come into proximity. The smaller object will begin to vibrate at the same frequency as the larger object, matching its oscillations. One example of entrainment can be seen in the synchronization of fireflies. When fireflies of different species come into proximity, they will begin to flash their light at the same rate. The fireflies will continue to flash at the same rate even when they are far apart from each other.

Another example of entrainment can be seen in the synchronization of circadian rhythms. Circadian rhythms are the daily fluctuations in biological processes that occur in response to the day-night cycle. When two individuals with different circadian rhythms are exposed to each other, their rhythms will begin to entrain.

This phenomenon can be harnessed to create some amazing effects. For example, doctors can use entrainment to help patients heal from injuries and illnesses faster by sending healthy signals to the body. In addition, entrainment can be used to improve mental and physical performance. Athletes can use entrainment to improve their reaction time, stamina, and even their recovery time from strenuous workouts. Students can use entrainment to improve their test scores and grades. And business professionals can use entrainment to improve their productivity and focus.

The discovery of entrainment goes back to the 17th century and is attributed to the research of

Dutch scientist Christiaan Huygens. Huygens was the first to discover that two pendulum-based clocks, when hung next to each other, would eventually begin to swing in unison. This phenomenon, now known as entrainment, was a revelation at the time, and set the stage for further discoveries in the field of synchronization.

It was not until nearly a century later that another major breakthrough in the understanding of entrainment occurred. In the early 19th century, French physicist Jean-Baptiste Joseph Fourier developed a theory that any arbitrary periodic functions could be represented as a sum of simple sine and cosine waves. This work laid the foundation for the field of harmonic analysis and is considered one of the most important contributions to mathematics and physics of the 19th century.

The next major milestone in the discovery of entrainment came in the late 1800s, with the work of German physicist Heinrich Hertz. Hertz was the first to show that electromagnetic waves could be used to induce synchronization in oscillating systems. This finding paved the way for the subsequent development of radio, television, and other forms of wireless communication.

Also, in the early 1920s, another German physicist named Walter Schottky made a pivotal contribution to the field of entrainment. Schottky showed that when two oscillating systems are coupled together, they will tend to synchronize with each other if they are close in frequency. This finding laid the foundation for the study of entrainment in biological systems.

The History of Brainwave Technology

In the 1950s, Robert Monroe, a radio engineer, began to experiment with brainwave entrainment. He found that certain frequencies could induce states of relaxation and sleep, and others could increase alertness and concentration. Monroe eventually founded The Monroe Institute in 1974 to help advance the research on brainwave entrainment. The Monroe Institute is now a leading provider of brainwave entrainment products and services.

In 1973, Gerald Oster published an article in Scientific American entitled "Auditory Beats in the Brain" which played a major role in bringing brainwave entrainment into mainstream awareness. In this article, Oster detailed his experiments with binaural beats and their effects on the brain. Oster found that when he played two different tones (one in each ear), the brain would produce a third tone, which was the result of their interaction with each other. Oster also found that the third tone produced by the brain could be used to alter the brain's state. For example, Oster found that he could induce a meditative state in his subjects by playing a binaural beat that was slightly below the alpha frequency. This research led to the development of light and sound machines commonly used in brainwave entrainment.

In 1986, the book *Megabrain* by Michael Hutchison popularized the idea of using light and sound machines for brainwave entrainment. The idea quickly caught on, and many companies began to sell their own versions of brainwave entrainment devices and methods, notably Centerpointe Research Institute that created Holosync and José Silva that created The Silva Method. While each company had their own devices and methods, they all shared the common goal of helping people change their brainwaves to improve their health and well-being.

Today, brainwave entrainment is more popular than ever. Thanks to advances in technology, there are now a variety of ways to experience it, from simple apps on your phone to sophisticated machines that can be used in a professional setting.

Brainwaves: The Rhythms of the Brain

Brainwaves are electrical impulses that travel through the brain produced by the firing of neurons, and can be measured by electrodes placed on the scalp. Brainwaves play an important role in regulating physical function, including heart rate, breathing, and metabolism; a role in cognitive functions, such as memory, learning, and attention; and a role in emotional regulation and control of one's level of consciousness. Brainwave patterns can also be used to diagnose and treat certain medical conditions, such as epilepsy and depression.

Since the 1970s, scientists have studied the effects of meditation on brainwave activity and have found that it can help to alter brainwave patterns in a variety of ways. Yinnergy is a type of meditation that can be beneficial for mental and emotional well-being by helping to change those patterns and improving brainwave function in a highly effective way.

There are several brainwave patterns that have been identified, but within the scope of this book, we will only focus on four major ones (beta, alpha, theta, and delta) plus three additional ones (epsilon, gamma, and lambda).

Beta Brainwaves

Beta brainwaves (13-30 Hz) are electromagnetic brain activity that occurs when we are alert and focused, and when we are actively engaged in using our senses or in mental activity such as problem-solving and decision-making. Beta brainwaves are also associated with concentration and cognitive function.

Research suggests that beta frequencies, associated with alertness and concentration, can have a positive impact on cognitive function. Studies, such as the ones published in the journal *Frontiers in Human Neuroscience* in 2014 and 2015, found that techniques such as tACS and tDCS applied at beta frequencies led to improved working memory performance in healthy adults. However, more research is needed to fully understand the underlying mechanisms and potential therapeutic applications of these techniques.

Other benefits of beta brainwaves include:
- Refined mental clarity and focus.
- Sharper thinking and improved memory.
- Enhanced problem-solving abilities.
- Greater creativity and better decision-making.
- Increased ability to pay attention.
- Improved hand-eye coordination.

Alpha Brainwaves

Alpha brainwaves (8-13 Hz) are associated with a state of calmness and wakeful relaxation in which you are alert and aware, but your mind is not taxed with mental activity. This is the state you are in when you are daydreaming. Many people find that they are more creative while in the alpha state and better able to learn. This is because alpha brainwaves give you better access to the right side of your brain, which is linked to creativity. When you are in an alpha state, you are also more open to new ideas and suggestions.

There are many ways to achieve alpha brainwaves. One way is through meditation, which allows you to quiet your mind and increase your alpha brainwaves. Other ways include doing relaxation exercises (such as yoga or Tai Chi), getting a massage, spending time in nature, practicing deep breathing exercises, and spending time in a sauna or steam room.

Other benefits of alpha brainwaves include:
- Greater imagination and productivity.
- Deeper focus and concentration.
- Improved memory and learning.
- Decreased stress and anxiety.

Theta Brainwaves

Theta brainwaves (4-8 Hz) are associated with deep meditation and prayer, and can facilitate more profound spiritual experiences. According to researchers such as Dr. Stanislav Grof and Dr. Michael A. Persinger, theta brainwaves offer a unique window into our spiritual lives. When we meditate or pray, we often enter a theta state in which we can experience a deep sense of peace and connection to the Divine. We are more open to receiving guidance from our higher selves and able to access greater levels of wisdom and insight.

The theta state is also associated with a deep sense of oneness with all creation, and love and compassion for all beings. We may also have experiences of transcendence where we feel a sense of unity with the cosmos, offering us a glimpse into the mystical and spiritual dimensions of reality.

Back in 2012, researchers from China and the United States confirmed that theta brainwaves were more common in people who were engaged in activities such as daydreaming and creative writing, compared to those who were engaged in more structured activities such as reading or math. Additionally, people who reported higher levels of creativity also had higher levels of theta activity in their brains.

Similar to alpha brainwaves, theta brainwaves also allow for:
- Greater imagination and productivity.
- Deeper focus and concentration.
- Increased sense of well-being and calmness.
- Relief from stress and anxiety.
- Improved sleep and restfulness.

Delta Brainwaves

Delta brainwaves (1-4 Hz) are associated with deep sleep, restorative healing, and dreaming. Given that the unconscious mind is thought to be most active in deep sleep, the delta frequencies embedded within the Yinnergy soundtracks may help one to access and influence it.

Delta brainwaves can help improve mental clarity and memory, as well as increase your ability to focus and concentrate; help reduce stress and anxiety while improving your overall mood and sense of well-being; and enhance your immune system to help fight off diseases. Delta brainwaves are also linked to the release of human growth hormone, which helps to repair and regenerate tissues.

Delta brainwaves are the second slowest of the seven brainwaves defined in this book. They are associated with the deepest level of relaxation and are important to:

- Increase the body's ability to heal.
- Protect the brain against the effects of aging.
- Relieve stress and increase immunity.
- Enhance creativity and memory.

Epsilon Brainwaves

Epsilon brainwaves (0.1-1 Hz) are some of the lowest frequency brainwaves and are also associated with deep meditation and prayer, similar to theta brainwaves. They are also the brainwave state of people during near-death experiences.

It is believed that epsilon brainwaves may be associated with hypnosis. Participants under hypnosis may be showing increased epsilon activity in the brain. However, more research is needed to confirm this connection and understand the underlying mechanisms of hypnosis. Some benefits of epsilon brainwaves are similar to the other types of brainwaves previously mentioned, including improved memory, focus, and concentration; increased creativity; enhanced sleep quality; reduced stress and anxiety; and greater feelings of well-being and calmness. They have been shown to improve healing after injuries and to boost the immune system.

Additionally, epsilon brainwaves have been associated with mystical experiences and altered states of consciousness, resulting in:
- Increased connection to the Divine.
- Greater clarity during meditation.
- Deeper understanding of spiritual concepts.
- Enhanced psychic abilities.

- Increased ability to heal oneself and others.
- Greater access to subconscious knowledge and the unified field.

Gamma Brainwaves

Gamma brainwaves (30-100 Hz) are a type of brainwave associated with high levels of mental activity and considered to be involved in the processing of information from short-term memory. They are also linked to higher states of consciousness, deep meditation, and prayer. Researchers such as Dr. Andrew Weil, Dr. Herbert Benson, and Dr. Jeffrey Schwartz believe that gamma brainwaves may be the key to unlocking the full potential of the human brain.

Studies have shown that people with higher levels of gamma activity tend to be more successful in various cognitive tasks, such as problem-solving and memory recall. There is also evidence that gamma brainwaves offer benefits such as higher levels of empathy and compassion, improved perception, and increased alertness. Some people believe, including myself, that gamma brainwaves can produce a state of heightened awareness and provide a person with a greater sense of connection to the world around them. Additionally, gamma brainwaves are believed to promote healing and well-being.

A gamma brainwave study published in February 2020 in the journal *Frontiers in Human Neuroscience* studied monks who had been practicing meditation for an average of 19 years, with over 27,000 hours of experience. The study found that when the monks were meditating, their brainwaves were mostly in the gamma range, with high levels of activity in the frontal and parietal lobes of the brain, which are associated with attention and self-awareness. The study shows that meditation can produce changes in brainwave activity that are associated with increased levels of focus and mental activity.

Lambda Brainwaves

Lambda brainwaves (100-200 Hz) are high-frequency brainwaves that are associated with peak concentration and mental clarity. Along with previously mentioned types of brainwaves, they also offer potential benefits such as improved focus, concentration, and memory; increased creativity and intuition; and enhanced well-being with lower stress levels and greater sleep quality. Additionally, lambda brainwaves have been associated with heightened levels of serotonin, a neurotransmitter that plays a role in mood regulation.

Other benefits of lambda brainwaves may include feeling more spiritually connected, more compassion and understanding towards others, and more interconnected with the universe as a whole and all that exists.

The Yinnergy Program

Yinnergy is an audio technology created in 2010 for personal growth, to produce meditative states of consciousness and to unify the body and mind through the work of meditation.

Yinnergy is designed to create changes in the listener's brainwave frequencies based on the principle of entrainment (the tendency of two oscillating objects to sync up with each other). When you listen to Yinnergy using headphones, your brainwaves begin to follow the frequencies of the audio signal and synchronize with it. This concept is similar to what happens when you listen to tribal drumming, through which the steady beat of the drums causes your brainwaves to fall in sync with the rhythm. These changes can create powerful effects on the mind and body, and potentially activate altered states of consciousness.

The Yinnergy program has 13+ levels (each with lower levels of carrier frequencies) and is designed for the meditator to progress through over time. The effects of Yinnergy are cumulative, which means that each successive level builds upon the effects of the previous ones.

When practicing with Yinnergy, the meditator will listen to the audio soundtrack every day, 7 days a week. The pre-level, which is called Yinnergy Purge, takes 4 to 6 months to complete, while the more advanced levels can take up to a year. It is not necessary to listen to all 13 levels to experience the benefits of the program. However, the more levels the meditator can progress through, the more profound the effects will be, and the more pronounced changes may become.

While they share similarities, there are some differences between Yinnergy and traditional meditation methods:

- Yinnergy uses binaural and monaural beats to help guide the meditator into a state of deep meditation, while traditional methods may use chanting, mantra repetition, or other techniques.
- Yinnergy allows meditators to achieve a deeper state of meditation in a shorter amount of time than with traditional methods, thanks to its use of constant high amplitude rhythm to hold the brain in a state of entrainment throughout the whole session.
- Yinnergy is easier to learn and quicker to master compared to traditional methods,

- Yinnergy is a more active form of meditation versus traditional methods, as it uses binaural beats and other forms of entrainment to stimulate different areas of the brain and help the meditator reach deep meditative states.

Yinnergy is available for download at https://true2soul.com/yinnergy.

The Benefits of Yinnergy

You may be asking, "What will Yinnergy do for me?" It will do a whole lot if you stick with it. Yinnergy meditation is more about powerful transformation as opposed to translation because it is a way to change your innermost being by dealing with the root cause. In this context, translation involves shifting your belief systems, ways of thinking, or perspectives, while transformation comes from direct experience. An apt analogy is that translation resembles rearranging the furniture in your apartment, while transformation is akin to relocating to an entirely new space on the floor above. The Yinnergy program is a way to access your true power and to create lasting change in your life. When you meditate, you are not just translating by having an altered state of consciousness, but transforming through actual change and evolving to reach one's full potential (hence Bodhi). You are creating new neural pathways in your brain that will lead to enhanced ways of thinking and being. It allows you to go beyond surface-level thoughts and emotions to access your true nature. It is a process of self-discovery that can lead to profound insights and changes in your life.

Yinnergy is an amazing tool that can help improve your life in many ways. It can help increase your focus and concentration, enhance your memory, boost your energy levels, and improve your mood by increasing levels of serotonin and dopamine, which are two neurotransmitters that are known to regulate emotions and anxiety. It is powerful and effective enough to help decrease certain symptoms of depression, cultivate happiness, and improve self-esteem.

It can also help reduce stress and anxiety, which promotes better sleep, improves digestion, decreases pain and inflammation, and enhances your overall sense of satisfaction. It can also support your spiritual development by cultivating peace and well-being, deepening your awareness, and strengthening your connection to higher self or God.

If you are looking for a way to improve your life and well-being, you may want to consider practicing with the Yinnergy program.

Yinnergy and PTSD

One of the goals of Yinnergy is to provide mentally and emotionally stimulating experiences that can help people improve their lives. Yinnergy can impact the brain in a way that may be helpful for people with PTSD by providing a safe and controlled environment in which to experience emotions and memories. By being able to control the environment, users may be able to work through their trauma in a more manageable way. Additionally, the audio experience may help to ground users and provide a sense of calm.

In a world that is often overwhelming and chaotic, Yinnergy may offer a much-needed respite. Some research has shown that binaural beats can help to improve focus and concentration, and it is possible that this could be beneficial for people with PTSD who often have difficulty with intrusive thoughts and flashbacks. This form of entrainment may also be helpful for people with PTSD who often experience high levels of anxiety and stress.

It is important to note that there is not yet a lot of research on the use of binaural beats for PTSD, and more research is needed to determine whether or not this is an effective treatment. However, the preliminary research that has been done is promising.

Yinnergy-Based Programs Within the School System

Yinnergy-based programs offer many potential benefits for students in the school system. These programs can help students to improve focus and concentration, increase academic performance, and reduce stress and anxiety. Additionally, Yinnergy-based programs can also promote positive social and emotional development, and provide an outlet for creative expression.

Within my field of practice, Yinnergy has been shown to improve cognitive function, increase IQ scores, and improve academic performance in children. I have worked with students from kindergarten to grade 12 and have seen significant improvements in reading comprehension, spelling, and math skills in a percentage of those who can use the technology regularly. The students also showed increased levels of concentration, motivation, and self-esteem. Yinnergy has also been shown to be beneficial for children with ADHD and autism. Some of the students who had access to the technology showed significant improvements in attention, impulsivity, and hyperactivity. The children who used Yinnergy also showed improved social skills, communication, and behavior. Yinnergy can be used by children of all ages, including children with mental and intellectual disabilities.

Yinnergy-Based Programs Within the Prison System

Inmates in the prison system could benefit greatly from Yinnergy-based programs. Yinnergy is successful in reducing negative impulses and behavioral issues in individuals. This technology works to synchronize the brain waves of the participants to create a more positive state of mind. When inmates are placed in a more positive state of mind, they are less likely to act out negatively or violently. In addition, Yinnergy has also been shown to improve cognitive function and reduce stress levels. This can be beneficial for inmates who are struggling with mental health issues or who have a history of trauma.

The Technologies Behind Yinnergy

As we have discussed, Yinnergy is based on the concept of brainwave entrainment (also known as binaural beats), which is the process of synchronization between two different wave forms. In this case, the brainwaves of the listener synchronize with the frequency patterns in Yinnergy, which can induce different states of consciousness through meditation.

Binaural Beats and Beat Frequencies

In the early 1800s, a Prussian experimenter named Heinrich Wilhelm Dove discovered that when he played two tones of slightly different frequencies into each ear, a pulsing or "beating" sensation would result.

But it was Dr. Gerald Oster, mentioned earlier, who found that when a person is exposed to a binaural beat, their brainwaves change to match the frequency of the beat. Binaural beats are now used for a variety of purposes, including relaxation, meditation, and focus.

The technology behind Yinnergy is made up of binaural beats (created from sine tones) to change brainwave activity. Binaural beats are an auditory illusion caused by two different tones of slightly different frequency that are played in each ear. When these two tones are combined, a third tone is perceived. This third tone is known as the beat frequency.

By playing binaural beats at different frequencies, you can alter your brainwave state and induce different states of consciousness. For example, if you play a binaural beat at a slower frequency (less than 25 Hz), you can induce a state of relaxation. However, if you play a binaural beat at a faster frequency (greater than 25 Hz but under 30 Hz), you can induce a state of alertness, or anxiety. By combining different frequencies of sound, you can generate a signal to influence the brain in multiple ways and create desired effects.

Yinnergy uses this form of entrainment to expose the brain to lower carrier frequencies. These frequencies are below the level of conscious awareness and penetrate deeper parts of the brain, and as such, help to keep the entrainment more effective for longer periods of time. Lower carrier frequencies can have a profound effect on the brain.

Through exposure to them, the brain can be trained to experience deeper states of whole-brain synchronization, meditation, and relaxation. In this way, lower carrier frequencies can reduce stress levels, improve concentration, balance the nervous system, boost the immune system, and enhance overall well-being.

This is another technology (called Subtle Energy Technology) used within Yinnergy that was added later in the program's development. We created a separate entrainment track which is in a state of destructive interference. This means that within this separate track, there are the two different energy fields working against each other, which cancels out the brainwave frequency activity of that very track. Though it cannot be heard by the human ear, and shows no activity, it can have a profound effect on the subtle bodies (as opposed to the actual brain and nervous system).

Sine Tones and Sine Waves

Sine tones are the foundation of the binaural beats embedded within the Yinnergy soundtracks. Sine tones are a type of sound wave characterized by a single frequency. This makes them distinct from other types of sound waves, which typically have multiple frequencies.

Sine tones are often used in music, sound design and effects, and audio production, as they can create a very pure and clean sound, and are used in many different types of music, including classical, electronic, and rock. Sine tones are created by a musical instrument or synthesizer that produces a tone with a very pure sinusoidal waveform, which is a smooth, repeating curve that has a definite pitch.

Sine tones are usually used as a part of a chord or as a solo tone. They can be used to create a wide range of sounds, from a gentle and soothing sound to a harsh and aggressive one. Sine tones can also be used to create a sense of space and depth in a piece of music.

Sine waves are a more complex sound wave that is made up of multiple frequencies. The main difference between a sine tone and a sine wave is that a sine tone is a pure tone that only consists of a single frequency, while a sine wave is a continuous wave that oscillates about a central value (or mean) and has a constant amplitude and wavelength. The function of a sine wave is to create a smooth, repeating signal that can be used to carry information.

Sine waves are one of the most basic and essential waveforms in existence. They are created when a vibrating object, such as a tuning fork, vibrates back and forth in a regular pattern. The resulting waveform will be a sine wave. Sine waves have interesting properties that make them highly effective in many contexts. One of the most important is that sine waves are easy to analyze mathematically, making them useful in signal processing and communications applications where precise analysis is required.

Another important property of sine waves is that they are naturally occurring waveforms, which means that they can be found in many places in the world around us. For example, sine waves are produced when a pendulum swings back and forth. Sine waves are also key in the study of waves and wave propagation. This is because sine waves have a very simple waveform that can be used to model more complex waveforms, making them an essential tool in the study of wave physics.

Pitch Frequencies and Carrier Frequencies

All sine tones possess their own pitch. A pitch is the perceived frequency of a sound and refers to the number of times per second that a specific sound wave vibrates. In the case of sine tones, the pitch is determined by the frequency of the tone: the higher the pitch, the higher the perceived frequency (and vice versa).

Pitch is influenced by several factors, including the frequency of sound waves produced by a vibrating object (the faster the vibration, the higher the pitch, and vice versa), the size of the vibrating object (the larger the object, the lower the pitch, and vice versa), and the tension of the object (the tighter the object, the higher the pitch, and vice versa).

With regard to binaural beats, a carrier frequency is the frequency of a waveform that results from the combination of a base frequency (which is the lower pitch frequency of the binaural beats) and the onset frequency (which is the higher pitch frequency). For instance, subtracting 211 Hz from 211.4 Hz yields 0.4 Hz as the beat frequency. Then, adding 211 Hz to 211.4 Hz, which totals 422.4, and dividing by 2, results in 211.2 Hz as the carrier frequency. This carrier frequency can be raised or lowered, but the beat frequency will remain at 0.4 Hz. The late Bill Harris of Centerpointe Research defined carrier frequencies as "the range of frequencies within which a signal can be varied without changing its basic characteristics." He would be referring to the beat frequencies.

Yinnergy utilizes low carrier frequencies to embed information within the brainwaves of the listener. This information is in sync with the brainwaves, which can subsequently produce changes in the listener's state of consciousness.

Delta Brainwaves and the Subconscious

The original Yinnergy program focuses on cultivating delta brainwaves in the listener. According to Dr. James Hardt, delta brainwaves are associated with leadership, charisma, and kundalini awakening. He states that delta waves allow us to access our unconscious mind, which is full of wisdom and knowledge. When we are in a state of delta brainwave activity, we are more likely to be open to new ideas and able to tap into our creative potential. This can be a very powerful state for making positive changes in our lives and achieving our goals.

People who can generate strong delta brainwaves tend to be natural charismatic leaders, with a strong ability to influence and inspire others, as these brainwaves are linked to a high level of focus and awareness. They also have a greater capacity for kundalini awakening, which is the activation of the body's dormant spiritual energy.

The kundalini is a spiritual energy that is said to reside at the base of the spine and, when awakened, rises up the spine and can cause a range of physical, mental, and emotional changes. Some people who have experienced a kundalini awakening report that they have also experienced an increase in delta activity, likely because the kundalini energy is activating the higher chakras (which are associated with delta activity).

Delta brainwaves are also linked to psychic abilities, such as clairvoyance and precognition. People who can access these abilities often have a higher level of delta activity as it is believed that they can access information and knowledge that is normally beyond our conscious awareness. While in delta, we are most open to receiving and processing information from the subconscious mind.

It is said that when a person is in delta, they can reach states of pure consciousness and bliss. There is anecdotal evidence (including my personal experience) that this can be facilitated through methods such as Shaktipat (a form of spiritual transmission in which the seeker is blessed with a sudden direct experience of Kundalini energy) or darshan (a form of blessing from a guru to a discipline through the act of sight). These experiences can be transformative, often resulting in profound changes in the seeker's consciousness and life.

While there is no scientific evidence behind these methods, they are understood and practiced in a variety of ways and spiritual traditions. Some gurus believe that they can transmit energy to their disciples through darshan. This energy is said to be able to induce delta brainwaves in the disciple and allow them to experience seeing the divine in all things and the unity in all of creation. This sense of unity is what allows us to experience the true nature of reality. When people are in the presence of a spiritual guru who is producing lots of delta brainwaves, they may feel a sense of peace and calm and increased feelings of love and compassion. They may also feel more connected to the guru and their message.

Yinnergy, with its high amplitude and low carrier frequency brain entrainment, is technically the auditory equivalent of being in a guru's presence, or of a Shaktipat transmission. This transmission of energy is said to cause a profound change in the consciousness of the recipient, leading to a higher state of awareness. The entrainment process of Yinnergy, produces a deep state of meditation that quiets the mind and can lead to bliss, and eventually to spiritual awakening.

When this technology is used daily, it can be used to access the subconscious, the unconscious, and the superconscious mind. It can allow you to tap into the vastness of Universal Consciousness and connect with the higher self, potentially leading to The Absolute of The Absolute (The Ground of All Being).

Vortex-Based Mathematics and Universal Patterns

The Mathematical Basis of Yinnergy's Algorithm

Yinnergy Meditation incorporates Vortex-Based Mathematics (which was created by mathematician Marko Rodin). The structuring of the binaural and monaural beats embedded within Yinnergy is based on this theorem, which makes it the most effective brainwave entrainment program available. When you meditate with Yinnergy, you are using a process that is based on the mathematical flow of the torus shape, which some consider to be the shape of the universe itself. This process is much more effective than other methods of brainwave entrainment because it is based on the essence of all things, which is represented by the magic number nine in Vortex-Based Mathematics. The Yinnergy technology is based on the theory that everything in the universe is of the same essence, and that this essence can be harnessed through sine waves to eventually create the state referred to as Bodhi.

Vortex-Based Mathematics is a revolutionary approach to math that integrates all the traditional fields of mathematics, but with a holistic, eastern perspective that is reminiscent of Vedic Mathematics. This approach to math goes beyond simple calculations and equations, and instead focuses on understanding the underlying patterns and principles that govern the universe. By utilizing a vortex-based framework, this form of math can provide a more intuitive and integrated understanding of mathematical concepts. It has the potential to transform the way we think about and engage with math and has already garnered significant interest from mathematicians and educators around the world.

To understand the mathematical formula behind the Yinnergy levels, it is important to understand the concept of brainwave entrainment and Vortex-Based Mathematics. Brainwave entrainment is a process in which the brain's frequency is influenced by external stimuli, such as sound or light. This can lead to changes in brainwave patterns and can affect the brain's activity and state of consciousness.

There are at least 13 levels of Yinnergy. Each level increases in amplitude which is a result of lower carrier frequencies. There are 72 tones comprising 36 onset and 36 base frequencies. But for the sake of not overwhelming you with too much information, we will only focus on 12 tones comprising of 6 onset and 6 base frequencies. As for the original 72 tones, these tones are organized into 6 groups of binaural beats, which are each made up of 18 monaural beats. The 3 6 9's represent empty channels that allow sound to interact and create sub-binaural rhythms, leading to an increase in the complexity of the human brain.

This revolutionary discovery combines the power of brainwave entrainment with the mysterious and mathematically perfect number 9, as represented in a branch of mathematics known as Polarized Fractal Geometry or Vortex-Based Mathematics. This type of mathematics is focused on the concept of using vortex patterns and fractals to better understand the fundamental nature of the universe and how it operates. By combining brainwave entrainment with this advanced form of mathematics, we can gain a deeper understanding of the way in which the brain functions and how we can harness its full potential. The potential applications of this discovery are vast, and could revolutionize the fields of mathematics, neuroscience, and personal development.

For more information about Vortex-Based Mathematics, please see the *Vortex-Based Mathematics Bonus Chapter* at the end of this book.

Levels of Yinnergy

There are several different versions of Yinnergy available and each one is designed to help the practitioner achieve certain goals by holding them within a specific frequency or range of frequencies (such as the alpha spectrum between 8 Hz and 13 Hz). Some versions are meant to help the practitioner relax and de-stress, while other versions help with focus and concentration. There are also versions that help the practitioner connect with their higher self or heal from past trauma. No matter what the goal, there is a Yinnergy meditation that can help the practitioner achieve it.

In the pre-level of Yinnergy which is called Yinnergy Purge, the focus is delta brainwaves. In this version, we take you from the beta brainwave state to alpha, then to theta within a 20-minute period, then take you into delta and hold you there for 40 minutes.

The official first, second, third and fourth level, which has lower carrier frequencies than Yinnergy Purge, is called Yinnergy Rise. Each level is divided up into four sub-categories, which are Yinnergy

Alpha, Theta, Delta, and Epsilon. Sub-categories 1 to 3 take about six months to complete, and level 4 takes up to a year.

The next four levels are called Yinnergy Harmony, which have lower carrier frequencies than Yinnergy Rise, and is also divided up into the same four sub-categories of Alpha, Theta, Delta, and Epsilon. It also takes at least a year to complete.

The next four levels are called Yinnergy Bliss, which have even lower carrier frequencies than Yinnergy Harmony It is also divided up into Alpha, Theta, Delta, and Epsilon and takes a least a year to complete.

After completing Yinnergy Bliss level 4, you have officially completed the whole Yinnergy program. But we do provide sub-levels for those who would like to experiment at the same carrier frequency as Yinnergy Bliss level 4, but at slower beat frequencies. These sub-categories contain two soundtracks of the default mode network, and two soundtracks of Iota, which takes another year at least to complete.

The Sub-Categories of the Yinnergy Levels

Yinnergy Alpha-Training

The focus of Yinnergy Alpha-Training is on alpha brainwaves, where we take you from high alpha brainwaves to low alpha for 40 minutes, theta for 10 minutes, then delta for 10 minutes. This version of Yinnergy specifically helps people to reach the alpha brainwave state (which is associated with increased relaxation and calmness, enhanced creativity and mental clarity, and greater focus and concentration).

Yinnergy Theta-Training

In Yinnergy Theta-Training, the focus is on theta brainwaves, where we take you from high alpha brainwaves down to low alpha for 10 minutes, then from high theta to low theta for 40 minutes, and then delta for 10 minutes. Theta brainwaves are associated with a state of deep meditation and prayer, and with the state of profound relaxation just before sleep. The theta state is also associated with the release of endorphins, which are hormones that promote a sense of well-being and heightened creativity.

Yinnergy Delta-Training

The Yinnergy Delta-Training is similar to Yinnergy Purge, but at a lower carrier-frequency. In this soundtrack, we take you from high alpha, then to theta within a 20-minute period, then take you into delta and hold you there for 40 minutes.

Delta brainwaves are one of the slowest and most elusive of the brainwave frequencies, ranging from 0.5 Hz to 4 Hz. They are typically associated with deep, dreamless sleep and a state of unconsciousness, but can also be present during moments of deep meditation and spiritual insight. Delta brainwaves are thought to be involved in the repair and restoration of the body and mind, and have been shown to have a number of potential health benefits, including reduced stress and anxiety, improved immune function, and enhanced relaxation and healing.

Yinnergy Epsilon-Training

For the Yinnergy Epsilon-Training, we take you from the high alpha brainwave state to low alpha for 10 minutes, theta for 10 minutes, delta for another 10 minutes, then hold you in epsilon for a 30-minute period.

Epsilon brainwaves are some of the rarest and most elusive of the brainwave frequencies, with a range of 0.5 Hz and below. These brainwaves are typically associated with a state of deep relaxation and meditation, and have been described as a "bridge between the conscious and unconscious mind." Epsilon brainwaves have been linked to a number of potential benefits, including reduced anxiety and stress, improved immune function, and increased feelings of peace and well-being.

Other Versions of Yinnergy

There are several different versions of Yinnergy meditation. Each one is designed to help the practitioner achieve a specific goal by holding them within a specific frequency, or within certain ranges such as Gamma or Lambda.

Yinnergy 2.0 (Gamma)

In Yinnergy Gamma-Training, the focus is on gamma and hyper-gamma brainwaves, where we take you into beta brainwaves for 10 minutes, then from gamma up to hyper-gamma for 40 minutes, and then lambda for 10 minutes. The gamma brainwave is one of the fastest brainwave frequencies, which starts at 40 Hz. Gamma waves are associated with the formation of long-term memories and retrieval of stored information in the brain. They are also responsible for processing sensory information and regulating consciousness, body movement, and coordination. Most people are not aware of the gamma brainwave state because it is usually only experienced during moments of peak mental and physical performance, or during times of intense concentration or meditation.

However, with the help of special audio technology, it is possible to train your brain to produce more gamma waves and experience the benefits of this state on a regular basis. Some of the benefits of entraining in gamma include increased mental clarity and focus, improved memory and recall, enhanced sensory processing, increased feelings of well-being and calmness, greater physical coordination and balance, boosted immune system function, and reduced stress and anxiety.

Yinnergy 2.1 (Lambda)

Yinnergy Lambda-Training is a practice designed for advanced practitioners, which aims to enhance the production of lambda brainwaves. These brainwaves are thought to be indicative of a high level of spiritual development, and are associated with individuals such as gurus, yogis, and enlightened beings. The goal of Yinnergy Lambda-Training is to help practitioners achieve this heightened state of consciousness. The training begins with 10 minutes in the beta brainwave state, followed by 10 minutes in gamma and hyper-gamma brainwaves, then 40 minutes in lambda brainwaves. Lambda brainwave entrainment is a powerful tool that can help you to achieve a variety of different goals including much deeper levels of improved focus and concentration, increased motivation and productivity, enhanced creativity and problem-solving ability, reduced stress and anxiety, and improved sleep quality.

Yinnergy Audio Coil

The Yinnergy Audio Coil is a modified version of the Rodin Coil, a 360-degree toroidal coil invented by Marko Rodin. This sine wave design is based on the mathematical principles of the coil's winding pattern, which involves wrapping the wiring every 12 or 15 degrees. This winding pattern is believed to amplify and intensify the flow of energy. The onset and base frequencies of the Yinnergy Audio Coil have been carefully selected to represent each degree of the design, resulting in a highly effective entrainment soundtrack.

Here is an example:

The resulting frequencies at each interval of t can be calculated using the equations above. For example, after 2.5 minutes (t = 2.5), the frequencies would be:

- $f_1(2.5) = 394 - 15(2.5) = 269$ Hz
- $f_2(2.5) = 390.8 - 15(2.5) = 265.8$ Hz
- $f_3(2.5) = 269 - 265.8 = 3.2$ Hz

To achieve the desired Audio Coil frequency pattern during the second half of the 1-hour session, the onset frequency is decreased by 15 Hz every 2.5 minutes until it reaches 214 Hz, while simultaneously decreasing the base frequency by 15 Hz every 2.5 minutes until it reaches 210.8 Hz. The beat frequency is maintained at 3.2 Hz for the duration of the 30-minute session.

The Yinnergy Audio Coil also comes in specialized versions of alpha, theta, delta, epsilon, gamma, and lambda.

Yinnergy Harmonics

$$f\_beat = (2^{\wedge}12 * 3.1\ Hz - 2^{\wedge}12 * 2.9\ Hz) / 2$$

Yinnergy Harmonics is another type of soundtrack used by advanced Yinnergy practitioners that involves the use of overtones, or harmonics, of two fundamental pitch frequencies: 3.1 Hz and 2.9 Hz. These frequencies combine to create beat frequencies of 0.2 Hz, 0.4 Hz, 0.8 Hz, 1.6 Hz, and so on. When the brain processes these frequencies, it creates a brainwave with an average frequency of 68.25 Hz, known as a hyper-gamma brainwave. Each level of a harmonic doubles in quantity, following a pattern of 1, 2, 4, 8, 7, 5 or 1, 2, 4, 8, 16, 32.

It is believed that incorporating harmonics into binaural beats can enhance the entrainment process. Harmonics create a more stable and consistent frequency, which allows the brain to follow the beat more easily. Additionally, resonance (the amplification of vibrations at a natural frequency) may improve overall brain function when harmonics are used in binaural beats.

An onset frequency of 3.1 Hz doubles in quantity 12 times, subtracting the base frequency of 2.9 Hz which also doubles in quantity 12 times simultaneously, averaging out to a beat frequency of 68.25 Hz.

Ultra-Sonic Yinnergy

Ultra-Sonic Yinnergy is a unique approach to sound therapy that uses high-frequency pitch frequencies (close to 20,000 Hz) that create beat frequencies to entrain certain areas of the brain and to stimulate the inner ear. This stimulation can improve communication and learning abilities, as well as reduce stress and anxiety.

Ultra-Sonic Yinnergy is based on the principle that the ear is the gateway to the brain, and that by stimulating the ear, we can directly impact the brain. Ultra-Sonic Yinnergy is also based on the principle that the ear is the primary organ of the body for receiving and processing information. The inner ear in particular is responsible for converting sound waves into electrical impulses that are sent to the brain. The brain then uses these impulses to interpret what we hear and to control our body's response to sound.

Yinnergy and Meditative Cross-Training

Yinnergy can be used as a stand-alone practice. But if you already work with spiritual or therapeutic practices (such as shadow work, sacred medicines, and shamanic practices), Yinnergy can support these by helping you access and work with the subtle bodies. These subtle bodies are considered the storehouse of our memories, emotions, and thoughts, and the source of our creative power. By working with these bodies, we can access our deepest wisdom and most creative potential, work through psychological challenges, connect with our higher selves and the wisdom of the ages.

Traditional Meditation

Traditional meditation practices have been used for centuries to promote relaxation, stress relief, mental and physical well-being, and even spiritual enlightenment. There are several different types of meditation, and many involve focusing the mind on a single point of attention, such as the breath, a mantra, or a visual object. Meditation can be done seated, lying down, or even walking. The goal is to clear the mind of distractions and to focus on the present moment.

Yinnergy meditation is a powerful program which can be used in conjunction with all traditional forms of meditation to help you achieve a deeper state of relaxation and concentration. By using specific sound frequencies to guide your brainwaves, Yinnergy can help you to focus on the present moment, leading to a more profound meditative experience.

Self-Enquiry and Contemplation

Self-enquiry is a process of turning inward and asking ourselves questions to gain a greater understanding of who we are, what we want, and how to achieve our goals. This process can be done through journaling, meditation, or simply taking some time to reflect on our lives. By getting to know ourselves better, we can learn how to better care for ourselves, clarify our values, and make choices that align with those values. When we engage in self-enquiry, we are turning our attention inward to examine our own thoughts, feelings, and beliefs. This process can be challenging, and it is often helpful to have a support system in place. Yinnergy can be a valuable tool for self-enquiry, as it helps to focus and calm the mind.

Self-enquiry can be a powerful tool for personal growth and transformation, and to help us identify and release old patterns and beliefs that no longer serve us. It can also help us to connect with our authentic selves and to develop a greater sense of self-awareness and self-compassion. Yinnergy can help to create a space of stillness and clarity within which we can explore ourselves more deeply.

Contemplation is another powerful tool for spiritual growth. This practice involves reflecting on your life and your relationship with the divine. It can help you gain a deeper understanding of your purpose and the meaning of your life. When you combine these two methods, you can create a powerful spiritual practice that can help transform your life.

Christian Contemplative Prayer

Yinnergy helps people achieve inner peace and harmony. When used in conjunction with Christian contemplative prayer (a form of prayer that is focused on silence, stillness, and contemplation), it can be an incredibly powerful tool for self-care and spiritual growth by helping to still the mind, body, and spirit and promoting a sense of peace and relaxation. When used regularly, it can help to improve overall mental and physical health.

Neuro-Feedback Training

This is a type of training that can improve meditation practice by providing feedback about brain activity. This feedback can help to improve focus and concentration, and to help identify areas of the brain that need more attention during meditation. There are different types of neuro-feedback training, and each has its own benefits for meditation practice.

Psychotherapy

Psychotherapy is a type of talk therapy that can be used to treat a wide range of mental health conditions. It involves talking to a trained therapist about your thoughts, feelings, and experiences to gain a better understanding of yourself and your problems. Psychotherapy can be an effective treatment for many mental health conditions, such as anxiety, depression, post-traumatic stress disorder (PTSD), and eating disorders. It can also be used to help people deal with difficult life events, such as bereavement, relationship problems, and redundancy.

Yinnergy can be used in conjunction with psychotherapy to help individuals heal from past trauma and achieve greater peace and well-being. When used together, these two modalities can help people to release emotions that are stuck in the body, connect with their authentic selves, and develop a more positive outlook on life.

Yinnergy can also help to ground and focus the mind, creating a space for stillness and reflection that can be beneficial in psychotherapy. It can help to improve mental and emotional clarity, providing a deeper understanding of oneself and others. It allows you to cultivate self-compassion and acceptance, two important qualities in healing from psychological distress. It can increase self-awareness, a key ingredient in successful psychotherapy. And it can promote relaxation and stress reduction, both of which are helpful in managing symptoms of anxiety and depression.

Breathwork

Breathwork is a powerful tool that can be used in conjunction with Yinnergy to help you achieve your desired state of consciousness. When used together, these two modalities can help you quickly and easily enter a state of deep relaxation, concentration, or sleep. Breathwork is a simple yet effective way to alter your state of consciousness. By changing the way you breathe, you can change the way you feel. There are many different types of breathwork, but the most common and easiest to learn is the 4-7-8 breath (by inhaling through your nose while mentally counting 4 seconds, holding for 7 seconds, then opening your mouth to exhale completely for 8 seconds). The 4-7-8 breath is a great way to quickly relax the body and mind and can be used whenever you need to de-stress or unwind. When used in conjunction with Yinnergy, the 4-7-8 breath can help you more easily enter and maintain a state of deep meditation.

Shadow Work

Shadow work is the process of bringing to light the parts of ourselves that we have hidden away in our subconscious. It is a way of coming to terms with the parts of ourselves that we are ashamed of, or that we have been trying to ignore. Shadow work can be difficult and painful, but it can also be liberating and empowering. It is a way of getting to know ourselves on a deeper level, and to learn to love and accept all of our aspects. When it comes to personal growth and development, there are many different approaches that one can take. Some people prefer to work on their shadow side, while others find that meditation is a more effective way to do so. However, Yinnergy is an approach that combines both these methods.

Yinnergy is a type of meditation that is specifically designed and incredibly effective to help individuals work on their shadow aspects when combined with shadow work practices, as it allows individuals to go deep within themselves to explore these hidden aspects. Often, individuals are afraid of their shadow side, as they may feel that it is something that is dark and negative. However, by working on this through Yinnergy and with a trusted practitioner, individuals can begin to integrate these aspects into a more holistic sense of being. In doing so, individuals can become more whole, well-rounded people who are able to lead more fulfilling lives. Some of the benefits of Yinnergy in conjunction with shadow work include:

- Improved self-awareness;
- Greater insight into one's own motivations, behaviors, and reactions;
- Deeper self-acceptance and self-compassion;
- Reduced negative emotions such as anxiety, anger and depression;
- Increased positive emotions such as happiness, peace and love;

- Deeper relationships with others;
- Greater clarity about life purpose and goals;
- Enhanced creativity and intuition;
- Increased physical and mental well-being.

Yinnergy and Physical Health

Throughout the years, my clients have mentioned that their health has improved and that they attribute this to Yinnergy. Our program does produce certain changes in brainwave activity, which may have an impact on physical health.

For example, Yinnergy can be effective at improving digestion and overall gut health by increasing the production of stomach acid, support the movement of food through the intestines, and reduce inflammation in the digestive tract.

Another example is that Yinnergy can help to reduce pain by changing the way that our neurons communicate with each other. The brain is made up of billions of cells called neurons, which communicate with each other through electrical impulses. When we experience pain, it is because our neurons are sending out electrical impulses which are interpreted by our brain as pain. By providing our brain with a different frequency of electrical impulses, Yinnergy can begin to change the way that the brain interprets these impulses. This can lead to a reduction in the amount of pain that we feel. Additionally, Yinnergy can also help to reduce pain by increasing the levels of certain chemicals in our brain. These chemicals, such as serotonin and dopamine, can help to reduce the perception of pain.

Yinnergy can also reduce inflammation by sending out specific frequencies that help to balance the body and reduce stress. Stress is a known trigger for inflammation, so by reducing it, our technology may help to reduce inflammation. Yinnergy can also help improve circulation and to help the body to detoxify, which may also help to reduce inflammation.

The Importance of Mindful Eating

As you move through the deeper levels of the Yinnergy program, you may naturally and intuitively start making changes in your diet, which is an important aspect of meditation for several reasons.

First, the food we eat can impact our physical well-being. Since meditation is an activity that requires physical stillness, it is important to be mindful of what we are putting into our bodies.

Second, what we eat can also impact our mental state. Since meditation is a practice that requires focus and concentration, it is important to be aware of how our diet affects our mind.

Lastly, the energy we put into our bodies through the food we eat can impact the energy we put out into the world. And since meditation is a practice of mindfulness and intention, it is important to be aware of how our diet affects our vibration.

Below are some examples of diets and foods that support our well-being, as well as ones that do not, keeping in mind that it is important to find out what works best for you while consulting with your health practitioner.

Organic/Plant-Based Diet

As you evolve spiritually, what you put in your body will be vital. New food options may be considered such as organic foods or a plant-based diet. Organic foods are grown without the use of synthetic pesticides, herbicides, or fertilizers, while plant-based diets are centered around consuming whole, unprocessed plant foods.

There are many reasons to choose organic foods. One reason is that they are free of harmful chemicals that can potentially damage your health. Eating organic foods has been linked with lower rates of cancer, heart disease, and other chronic illnesses. Another reason to choose organic foods is that they are more nutrient-dense than their non-organic counterparts which means that they provide more vitamins, minerals, and antioxidants that are essential for good health.

A plant-based diet also has many benefits for your health. Studies have shown that plant-based diets can lower your risk of heart disease, stroke, cancer, diabetes, and other chronic illnesses. Plant-based diets are also associated with lower rates of obesity.

Following an organic diet and plant-based diet can help to improve the overall quality of your life. Eating nutritious foods that make you feel good and give you energy can help you to be more productive, creative, and happy.

The Ayurvedic Diet

The Ayurvedic diet is a holistic approach to health that originated in India and focuses on balancing the mind, body, and spirit. This balance is thought to promote a sense of well-being and inner peace. This ancient system of medicine is based on the belief that good health is achieved when the three doshas (vata, pitta, and kapha) are in balance. When all three doshas are balanced, it is said to promote good health, vitality, and inner peace.

However, it is important to note that the Ayurvedic diet is just one aspect of a holistic approach to health and well-being, and may not be suitable for everyone. It is important to consult with a healthcare professional or Ayurvedic practitioner before making any changes to your diet.

Other Dietary Considerations

Onions and Garlic

In the traditional Hindu dietary classification, onions and garlic are considered "tamasic" foods. Tamasic foods are thought to be heavy, dull, and inactive, and are believed to create negative vibrations in the body and mind. They are believed to promote laziness, sleep, and ignorance, which are incompatible with the goals of meditation and spiritual practices.

Hinduism, Jainism, Buddhism, and some schools of yoga all consider onions and garlic to be tamasic foods that can disrupt the subtle energies of the body and mind, making it harder to focus and concentrate during meditation. These traditions also place a strong emphasis on non-harming and ahimsa (non-violence) and may avoid onions and garlic because they are believed to harm and disturb the consciousness of the plant when they are harvested.

It is important to note that these beliefs about onions and garlic are based on traditional teachings and may not be supported by modern scientific evidence. Ultimately, the decision to include or exclude onions and garlic from the diet is a personal choice that should be made based on individual preferences and needs.

Additionally, the Ayurvedic tradition considers onions and garlic to be Pitta-aggravating foods that can increase heat in the body and potentially cause health problems such as indigestion, heartburn, acid reflux, ulcers, skin rashes, acne, excess body heat, and insomnia. If you are prone to Pitta imbalances, it may be advisable to avoid onions and garlic in your diet. However, as mentioned, it is important to consult with an Ayurvedic practitioner or healthcare professional before making any changes to your diet.

Distilled Water

There are many reasons why it is believed that distilled water is important for meditators. Distilled water is pure water that has had all impurities removed from it. This means that it is free of toxins, chemicals, and other contaminants that can be found in tap water. This makes it the ideal water for meditation, as it will not interfere with your practice. In addition, it is believed that distilled water has a high energy vibration that can help to raise your own energy vibration, making it easier to reach a state of meditation. It can also help to cleanse and purify your aura, which can improve your meditative experience.

Distilled water is also important for meditators because it can help to promote a sense of calm and peace. When you are feeling anxious or stressed, drinking distilled water can help to ease those feelings. Overall, distilled water is an important part of a meditator's toolkit by helping to purify your body and mind, and promote a deeper meditative experience.

Flour and Sugar

There are many reasons one should reduce their intake with refined sugars and white flour, but for meditators, two stand out above the rest.

First, these foods can lead to spikes in blood sugar levels, which in turn can lead to feelings of anxiety and irritability, causing distraction during meditation.

Second, refined sugars and white flour can promote inflammation in the body, which can contribute to pain and stiffness in the joints, making it difficult to sit still for long periods of time.

The Top 7 Nootropics

Nootropics are substances that can be taken to improve cognitive function, including memory, focus, attention, and motivation. Nootropics can either be natural or synthetic. We believe that taking certain nootropics while using Yinnergy can enhance the effects of meditation by improving focus and attention, and relaxing the mind and body.

Some natural nootropics that may be complementary to Yinnergy include:

- **Gotu Kola:** Also known as Centella asiatica, gotu kola is an herb that has been traditionally used in Ayurvedic and Chinese medicine for centuries. The leaves of the plant are often consumed as a tea, and the extract is commonly used in skincare products. Recent studies have shown that gotu kola may help to improve cognitive function and memory, as well as reducing stress and anxiety. These effects are thought to be due to the herb's ability to increase blood circulation and promote nerve growth. Gotu kola is also said to be beneficial for meditation, as it can help to still the mind and promote a state of calm.

- **L-Theanine:** This amino acid is found in green tea and is known for its calming and relaxing effects. It may help to ease anxiety and improve sleep quality.
- **Bacopa Monnieri:** This nootropic herb is traditionally used in Ayurvedic medicine to enhance memory and cognitive performance. It is thought to work by increasing levels of the neurotransmitter acetylcholine in the brain.
- **Ginkgo Biloba:** This popular nootropic herb is derived from the Ginkgo biloba tree. It is thought to improve cognitive function by increasing blood flow to the brain.
- **Rhodiola Rosea:** This herb is traditionally used in Russian and Scandinavian folk medicine to counteract fatigue and enhance physical and mental performance. It is thought to work by increasing levels of the neurotransmitters dopamine and norepinephrine in the brain.

- **Ashwagandha:** Another herb used in Ayurvedic medicine, ashwagandha is thought to help reduce stress and promote relaxation.
- **Panax ginseng:** This nootropic herb is derived from the Panax ginseng plant. It is traditionally used in Chinese medicine to enhance energy and stamina, and is thought to improve cognitive function by reducing levels of the stress hormone cortisol in the brain. It is important to note that this nootropic should not be used with entheogens as it may increase the risk for certain side effects, such as anxiousness, headache, restlessness, and insomnia.

Physical Activity

Meditation has been used for centuries to promote relaxation, peace of mind, and self-awareness. In recent years, meditation has gained popularity in the western world as a stress-reduction technique. A growing body of scientific research is beginning to explore the potential health benefits of meditation, including its effects on physical activity.

A recent study published in the journal *Frontiers in Human Neuroscience* concluded that physical activity may impact the way our brains respond to meditation. The study found that people who were physically active had increased levels of activity in the prefrontal cortex and hippocampus, two regions of the brain associated with attention and memory. The study participants who were physically active also had greater levels of connectivity between the two regions. This research suggests that physical activity may enhance the effects of meditation on the brain. The findings are preliminary, but they offer a potential explanation as to why meditation has been shown to improve mental health and well-being.

Yoga

Yoga is an ancient system of physical and mental development that originates in India. The word yoga comes from the Sanskrit root "Yuj", meaning "to yoke" or "to unite."

Yoga is a system of discipline that includes breath control, simple meditation, and the adoption of specific bodily postures. Different styles of yoga offer different benefits to the Yinnergy practice. For example, Hatha yoga emphasizes physical postures and breathing exercises to purify the body and calm the mind, while Vinyasa yoga focuses on linking breath with movement to build heat and create fluidity in the body. Kundalini yoga incorporates chanting, meditation, and breathing exercises to awaken energy and consciousness, while Bikram yoga is a series of 26 postures performed in a heated room to detoxify and cleanse the body. Each of these styles of yoga offer unique benefits that can support and enhance the Yinnergy meditation practice.

Walking

According to a recent scientific study published in 2020 in the Journal of Alzheimer's Disease, walking regularly enhances meditation practice. Also, research published in the journal *Frontiers in Psychology*, found that people who walk regularly are more likely to experience positive changes in their meditation practice, including increased focus and concentration, and improved mental well-being. The study was conducted by a team of researchers from the University of Arizona and the University of California, San Diego that asked participants to walk for 30 minutes a day, three times a week, for a total of eight weeks. The participants were also asked to meditate for 20 minutes a day, five times a week. The researchers found that the participants who walked regularly experienced significant improvements in their meditation practice, including increased focus and concentration, and improved mental well-being. In addition, the participants who walked regularly also reported feeling more connected to and aware of their surroundings during their meditation practice.

Cardiovascular Training

Cardiovascular training also enhances meditation practice, according to recent scientific research, through a study published in the journal *Frontiers in Psychology*. Cardiovascular exercise can help increase focus and attention, two key components of successful meditation. In addition, cardiovascular training can help to reduce stress and anxiety, which can make it easier to enter a meditative state. By incorporating cardiovascular exercise alongside your Yinnergy meditation practice, you can improve your overall health and well-being.

Weight Training

There is a growing body of scientific research that suggests that weight training can enhance meditation practice. A recent study published in the Journal of Strength and Conditioning Research found that just eight weeks of weight training can significantly improve mindfulness meditation scores.

Other research has found that weight training can help to improve focus, concentration, and mental clarity, while reducing stress and anxiety levels. All these benefits can make it easier to meditate effectively.

Yinnergy and Emotional Health

Yinnergy is a form of meditation that helps people to become more aware of their thoughts and feelings, and to learn to regulate them more effectively by raising your emotional and mental thresholds. This allows you to better handle stress, anxiety, and other difficult situations. Yinnergy can also help you become more emotionally and mentally resilient, which supports a more successful and fulfilling life (including enlightenment).

Yinnergy can help increase levels of happiness and well-being by changing brainwave patterns, but it is important to clarify that this is not what people generally recognize as happiness. In this context, happiness is a state of contentment that does not rely on anything external.

In addition, Yinnergy helps to rewire the brain for increased levels of bliss known in the east as Satcitananda. This is a Sanskrit word meaning "existence-consciousness-bliss" and a concept in Hinduism that refers to the "blissful, supreme Reality" that is the ultimate goal of life. It is a state of consciousness beyond the ordinary waking, dream, and deep sleep states and is considered the highest state that can be attained. To experience Satcitananda, one must first go through the process of self-realization, which results in a direct consciousness of the true nature of the Self. There are many paths that can be taken towards this experience (such as yoga, meditation, and service to others), but once the Self is realized, the individual will be able to experience the blissful, supreme Reality that is Satcitananda.

Yinnergy and Mental Health

Yinnergy can help give you the mental edge you need to be successful in whatever you do. This audio technology entrains the brains by creating slower, synchronized brainwave patterns to generate desired mental states.

When used with headphones, it can help to improve focus and concentration by providing the brain with a more stable and efficient environment in which to function. Given that the brain is constantly bombarded with information and distractions from the outside world, it can be difficult to filter out the noise, concentrate effectively, and focus on what is important. Yinnergy helps to reduce the amount of information that the brain needs to process by creating a more efficient and focused state of mind, which also results in improved memory.

Yinnergy is also a stress reduction tool that deeply supports the listener to reach a state of deep relaxation. The patterns embedded in the soundtracks are therapeutic, and can help to reduce stress and anxiety, improving sleep as a result.

Yinnergy is an effective way to enhance levels of awareness, which is the ability to be aware of one's surroundings and oneself at the same time, or ultimately, becoming aware that the one-self is and always will be the All that is beyond and includes all surroundings.

There are many benefits to having more awareness, and Yinnergy is one of the best ways to develop this skill. You become more in tune with your environment, can more easily spot potential dangers, and can better understand and interpret the behavior of those around you. Yinnergy is an excellent way to develop awareness because it helps you to focus and concentrate on your surroundings, allowing you to notice things that you would otherwise miss.

In addition, Yinnergy is a powerful tool to help you develop your intuition. Intuition is a form of super awareness that allows you to know things without knowing how or why you know them. Developing your intuition can be extremely helpful in many situations because it can give you information that you would not otherwise have.

Yinnergy can also help to relieve suffering of all kinds because it is a form of entrainment that can help change the brainwave patterns of those who use it, leading to a more positive and optimistic state of mind. According to ancient wisdom, resistance is the cause of all suffering because it is the root of it. When we resist what is, we are in a state of dis-ease. When we are resisting what is happening in the present moment, we are resisting our own true nature. We are resisting the flow of life. Resistance is the cause of all suffering because it keeps us from being present. When we are present, we are in the flow of life itself. When we are in harmony with what is, we become the very presence of harmony.

Yinnergy and Spiritual Health

Yinnergy is a non-invasive audio technology that uses binaural beats to help the brainwave activity to become more coherent, which leads to a sense of calm, well-being, and mindfulness.

Numerous studies have shown that the practice of mindfulness meditation is beneficial for overall health and well-being. It can help reduce stress, anxiety, and depression, decrease pain, and improve sleep quality.

On a personal level, Yinnergy helps to cultivate positive emotions and states of mind; improve self-confidence and self-esteem while reducing self-sabotage; enhance relationships by promoting feelings of empathy, compassion, and understanding; and heal emotional traumas.

Yinnergy can also help improve connection to higher self or what some refer to as God by synchronizing the left and right hemispheres of the brain and develop their ability to communicate together.

The Fourth State of Consciousness

When speaking about higher self or God in this context, I am referring to the fourth state of consciousness (also known as Turiya), which is a state of pure awareness beyond the other three states of waking, dreaming, and deep sleep. This is an experience of pure consciousness, beyond the mind, where there is no thought or mental activity whatsoever. This state is often referred to as "thoughtless awareness" or "pure consciousness" through which the true nature of reality is experienced because the mind is free from the veils of thought and perception.

When the mind is free from thought, you can see things as they truly are. Yinnergy produces changes in brainwave activity that can lead to this state. By gradually exposing the listener to different frequencies of sound in turn. This causes the brain to produce more of the desired frequency until it becomes second nature.

This powerful tool can help one to reach the fourth state of consciousness by creating specific brainwave patterns that encourage the brain to function in a more coherent state. When used consistently and with progress through the deeper levels of the program, Yinnergy can entrain the brain to the desired frequency and potentially allow the listener to eventually experience this fourth state of pure being.

The Fifth State of Consciousness

In addition to the fourth state of consciousness, there is a fifth state of consciousness that is sometimes referred to as "the stateless state" or "the pinnacle of all states". This level of consciousness is the state of absolute nondual suchness, also known as Turiyatitta (which simply means beyond the fourth). In this state, there is the direct knowing of oneness with all that is. It is often described as a state of absolute pure awareness characterized by unity consciousness, where one is not identified with any particular thought, feeling, or object, yet one finally realizes that they all these things and more simultaneously. This state is the goal of many spiritual traditions. From direct experience, I can say that Yinnergy allows the listener to reach higher states of consciousness and can be used as a tool to achieve this nondual state of pure suchness.

Attempting to reach this state has its challenges, so some people may experience the nondual state while using Yinnergy or by other means, while others may not; there is no guarantee. However, many people have found it to be a valuable tool in their journey to spiritual enlightenment.

The Seven Bodies of Manifestation

Distinct from the physical one, the subtle body (or bodies) is a concept in many spiritual traditions, including yoga, tantra, and Chinese medicine. It is often described as an energy field or aura that surrounds and interpenetrates the physical body. Though most of us may not be able to see them, this does not mean they do not exist, and they can be experienced.

In the yogic traditions, it is said that there are five or six subtle bodies which surround and interpenetrate the physical body, connected to it through the chakras. Each of these bodies is made up of a different kind of energy, and each has its own specific functions. The subtle bodies are responsible for our ability to perceive and interact with the world around us on a non-physical level.

Yinnergy can enhance our connection to the chakras and the subtle bodies by bringing them into alignment, clearing blockages in them, and promoting healing. When the subtle bodies are in balance, we are able to function at our highest level and connect with our true nature.

I will be giving a brief description of these subtle bodies in general terms to show how Yinnergy works with them.

The Gross Body

The gross body is the physical body that is visible to the naked eye, and is composed of the five elements: earth, water, fire, air, and ether. Yinnergy can enhance the gross body in some ways, as it is a non-invasive form of energy medicine that helps to improve the flow of energy in the body. This contributes to the overall health and well-being of an individual by improving sleep quality, reducing stress and anxiety, enhancing circulation and the immune system, and decreasing pain.

The Etheric Body

The etheric body is the energy body that surrounds and interpenetrates the physical body. It is the body of life force, also known as chi or prana. When you meditate using Yinnergy, you connect with the ether body and the life force energy that flows through it. This enhances the ether body and strengthens its connection to the physical body. The ether body is like a battery that stores energy. When it is strong and healthy, it can hold more energy and release it more effectively. This is why meditation is so beneficial for overall health and well-being.

The Astral Body

Probably one of the more popular templates is the astral body. The astral body is an invisible double of the physical body that is said to be the vehicle of the soul. To practice Yinnergy, it is important to first understand what the astral body is and the role it plays.

When the astral body is healthy and balanced, it is said to be able to move freely in and out of the physical body. It is also said to be able to travel to other planes of existence and interact with other beings.

Yinnergy is beneficial for the astral body because it helps to strengthen and balance it. It is also said to help purify the astral body of any negative energy that may be attached to it.

The Emotional Body

The emotional body is another layer of the aura and is said to hold information about a person's emotional state. In the yogic tradition, the emotional body is said to be one of the most important aspects of our being. It is said to be the storehouse of our emotions and the source of our power. The emotional body is also said to be the bridge between our physical and spiritual bodies.

Yinnergy is a great way to enhance the emotional body because it allows us to release any trapped emotions that are no longer serving us. This type of meditation can also help to increase our emotional awareness, which can lead to a deeper understanding of our own emotions.

According to the late author Louise Hay, physical symptoms are often the manifestation of unconscious thoughts, feelings, and emotions that are not fully acknowledged or processed. When one listens to Yinnergy over time, it is not uncommon for repressed or disowned material to come to the surface through various channels, including thoughts, feelings, emotions, and even physical symptoms such as aches, addictions, anxiety, and more. It is important to remember that this process is natural and necessary for personal growth, and there is nothing to be afraid of or concerned about. If any of these symptoms occur, it is important to become the witness and allow them to be expressed without personal judgement.

Here is a list of possible symptoms that may occur as the unconscious material resurfaces:

- **Aches:** These may be related to a longing for love or a desire to be held.
- **Addictions:** These may be a way of running from the self or a result of fear, or a lack of self-love.
- **Anxiety:** This may indicate a lack of trust in the flow and process of life.

- **Appetite, Excessive:** This may be related to fear or a need for protection, or a tendency to judge emotions.
- **Back Pain:** This may be a sign of a lack of emotional support or feelings of being unloved, or a reluctance to give love.
- **Back Curvature:** This may be a result of an inability to flow with the support of life, or a lack of trust in life and a lack of integrity or conviction.
- **Colds:** These may be a result of having too much going on at once or mental confusion and disorder, or may be a response to small hurts.
- **Crying:** Tears are a natural response to both joy and sadness, as well as fear.
- **Diarrhea:** This may be related to fear or rejection, or a desire to run away.
- **Dizziness:** This may be a result of flighty or scattered thinking, or a refusal to look at something.
- **Vomiting:** This may be a sign of a violent rejection of ideas or a fear of the new.
- **Headaches:** These may be a result of invalidating the self, self-criticism, or fear.
- **Hyperactivity:** This may be related to fear, feeling pressured or frantic, or a lack of control.

- **Insomnia:** This may be caused by fear, a lack of trust in the process of life, or guilt.
- **Itching:** This may be a sign of desires that go against the grain or a feeling of dissatisfaction or remorse, or a desire to get out or escape.
- **Migraine Headaches:** These may be a result of a dislike of being driven, resistance to the flow of life, or sexual fears.
- **Nausea:** This may be caused by fear or a rejection of an idea or experience.
- **Nervousness:** This may be related to fear, anxiety, struggle, or a lack of trust in the process of life.
- **Pain:** This may be a sign of guilt, as guilt often seeks punishment.
- **Pimples:** These may be a result of small outbursts of anger.
- **Rash:** This may be a sign of irritation over delays or an immature way of seeking attention.
- **Fatigue:** This may be a sign of resistance, boredom, or a lack of love for what one does.

The Mental Body

When we talk about the mental body, we are referring to the part of us that is responsible for our thoughts, and all other mental processes. The mental body is the part of us that is the most changeable and the most difficult to control. However, through listening to Yinnergy daily, we can learn to control our mental body and use it to our advantage. When we meditate, we are training our mental body to let go. This process is not easy, and it takes time and practice to master. However, the rewards are well worth the effort.

The Causal Body

The causal body is one of the subtle bodies in yogic tradition. It is said to be the body of karma, or the body of cause and effect. The causal body is said to be the source of our karma, and it is the body that determines our destiny. When we engage in regular practice using Yinnergy, we are working to enhance this causal body. This is the body that is responsible for our actions, and it is also the body that is most close to the divine. By working to improve the causal body, we can improve our karma and move closer to what we call Bodhi.

The Nondual Body

The nondual body is the highest state of being. It is a state of pure consciousness, beyond all thought and emotion. The nondual body is the ultimate reality, the True Self and the no-self. Yinnergy increases access and enhances the experience of the nondual body by quieting the mind, providing a deeper connection to the innermost parts of the self, and to the world around you. This type of meditation can lead to a more profound understanding of the true nature of reality...all of reality.

Kundalini, Chakras, and the Nadis

Yinnergy is an effective practice that can help to activate kundalini energy, open the chakras, and clear the nadis. When meditation is used and done correctly, it can be a powerful tool for spiritual growth and development.

Kundalini Awakening

As spoken earlier, kundalini is a spiritual energy that is located at the base of the spine. When this energy is awakened, it rises up the spine and through the chakras, or energy centers, of the body. Yinnergy is powerful enough to awaken kundalini. Yinnergy uses specific tones and frequencies to open the chakras and bring about deep states. As the chakras open and the mind frees itself, kundalini can begin to rise. Yinnergy can be an intense experience for some, so it is important to be well prepared.

Kundalini syndrome is a set of physical, mental, and emotional symptoms that can occur as a result of Yinnergy or other meditative practices. While kundalini syndrome can have both positive and negative effects, which can range from mild to severe such as increased energy levels, heightened sense of awareness, intensified emotions, increased spiritual awareness, and psychological and physical changes, it is important to be aware of these potential issues before undertaking any meditation practices. Some of the more common symptoms of kundalini syndrome include:

Positive Symptoms:
- Heightened awareness
- Increased sense of well-being
- Improved mental clarity
- Increased physical energy
- Improved sexual function
- Enhanced levels of creativity
- Psychic abilities

Negative Symptoms:
- Anxiety
- Depression
- Insomnia
- Irritability

- Dizziness
- Headaches
- Nausea
- Physical problems

While the negative symptoms can be challenging, the positive ones are what make the challenge well worth it. The main goal of kundalini syndrome is to help us become more aware of our spiritual nature and to connect with the divine energy that lies within us all.

The Chakras

Chakras are energy centers in the body that are responsible for our physical, mental, and emotional well-being. There are seven main chakras, each located along the spine. These chakras are the root chakra, sacral chakra, solar plexus chakra, heart chakra, throat chakra, third eye chakra, and crown chakra. Each chakra has its own unique energy and purpose. When our chakras are balanced, we feel healthy and happy. When they are out of balance, we may feel physically or emotionally unwell. Yinnergy can help to balance the chakras. It works by creating a "frequency following response" in the brain, which helps to promote a sense of calm and well-being. When the chakras are in balance, it is easier to maintain physical, emotional, and mental health. Some of you may or may not know this but there is a lot of debate surrounding the exact nature and function of the chakras. But most people can agree that they are energy centers located throughout the body.

Yinnergy is a technology that helps balance the chakras by providing the right stimuli. By using algorithms of Vortex-Based Mathematics, this entrainment helps the brainwave frequencies to become more aligned with those of the chakras, which can help to encourage balance and flow within them.

Brainwave entrainment experts hypothesize that entrainment may support the balancing of the chakra system. Some studies have shown that participants had significant increases in self-reported measures of physical, mental, and emotional well-being after using brain entrainment, which are directly related to the chakras. While more research is needed to confirm the specific effects of brain entrainment on the chakras, it is a promising technology that may be worth exploring if you are looking for ways to improve your chakra balance.

Root Chakra/Muladhara

Yinnergy is an effective tool for improving the root chakra. This chakra is located at the base of the spine and is responsible for our sense of security and stability. When it is out of balance, we may feel anxious, disconnected, and unsafe. Yinnergy can help to rebalance the root chakra by providing a deep sense of relaxation and calm. This can help to reduce anxiety and feelings of insecurity. In addition, Yinnergy can help to increase our sense of connection to the world around us. This can help us to feel more grounded and stable.

Sacral Chakra/Svadhisthana

The sacral chakra is the second chakra from the bottom of the seven chakras. It is located in the lower abdomen just below the navel. The sacral chakra is responsible for our creativity, sexuality, and passion, all of which Yinnergy can enhance by helping us to relax and let go of our inhibitions.

Solar-Plexus/Manipura

The solar plexus chakra is located just below the breastbone and is associated with the element of fire. This chakra governs our personal power, will, and confidence. When it is in balance, we feel in control of our lives and our destiny. When it is out of balance, we may feel powerless, weak, and uncertain. Yinnergy balances the solar plexus chakra by helping us to connect with our personal power and to tap into our inner strength. It also helps us to release any fears or doubts that may be holding us back from achieving our full potential. As we let go of these negative emotions, we open ourselves up to new possibilities and opportunities.

Heart Chakra/Anahata

Yinnergy is known to be very effective in opening and balancing the heart chakra. The heart chakra is associated with love, compassion, and the ability to connect with others on a deep level. When this chakra is balanced, one is able to give and receive love freely and easily, and experience a sense of inner peace and contentment. Working on this chakra creates a deep sense of connection and oneness with all of life. This allows for a more open and loving relationship with others, to be more empathetic, and to have a more compassionate outlook on life.

Throat Chakra/Vishuddha

Yinnergy is said to improve the throat chakra by stimulating the production of neurotransmitters and helping to regulate the endocrine system. The throat chakra is associated with communication, self-expression, and the ability to speak one's truth. It is said that when this chakra is balanced, one can communicate clearly and authentically, and express themselves without fear of judgment. It is also related to the thyroid gland, which controls metabolism and energy levels.

Third-Eye Chakra/Ajna

The third-eye chakra is the sixth chakra and is located between the eyebrows. This chakra is associated with intuition, insight, and imagination. It is said to be the center of perception and consciousness, responsible for the ability to see beyond the physical realm and access higher levels of understanding. Yinnergy can help to improve the third-eye chakra by increasing the flow of energy to this area. By doing so, it can help to improve intuition and insight, and can also help to improve imagination. This can lead to a more profound understanding of oneself and the world around us.

Crown Chakra/Sahasrara

The crown chakra is the energy center located at the top of the head. It is associated with the element of spirit and is considered the most spiritual of all the chakras. The crown chakra is said to be the connection between the physical body and the spiritual realm. Yinnergy is beneficial for the crown chakra as it helps to align and balance the energy center by helping to improve the flow of energy and communication between the physical body and the spiritual realm.

The Nadis

Nadis, or subtle energy channels, are the channels through which the life force or prana flows. There is said to be 72,000 nadis in the human body but that only a few are of significance. The three main nadis are the ida, pingala, and sushumna.

The ida nadi is associated with the moon and the left side of the body. It is said to be cooling and calming, and is responsible for our emotions and intuition. The pingala nadi is associated with the sun and the right side of the body. It is said to be energizing and stimulating, and is responsible for our mental activity and willpower.

Yinnergy is an effective method for refining the brain and nervous system because of the lower carrier frequencies embedded within its technology. This practice helps to purify the nadis and to improve the quality of one's thoughts and emotions. When they are blocked or constricted, it can lead to physical and mental health problems. Yinnergy uses sound frequencies to vibrate and open these nadis, allowing the free flow of energy and promoting health and well-being. This flow of energy is said to help break up any blockages that may be present due to past traumas.

Yinnergy and the Thinking Mind

The Multiple Intelligences Theory

If you have never heard about The Multiple Intelligences theory, this theory was first proposed by Dr. Howard Gardner back in 1983. This theory suggests that there are eight different types of intelligence that can be identified in humans, which are: logical-mathematical, spatial, musical, kinesthetic, interpersonal, intrapersonal, linguistic, and naturalistic.

We now know that there are even more types of intelligences that humans possess. Every intelligence has its own unique way of processing information and each one is important in its own way. Yinnergy has been shown to improve all these intelligences at different scales of development.

Logical-Mathematical Intelligence

Entrainment programs, such as Yinnergy, are a simple yet powerful form of meditation that can be used to enhance logical and mathematical intelligence. The basic principle behind Yinnergy is that by focusing on the two hemispheres of the brain, one can still the mind and achieve a greater state of clarity and insight. This allows the individual to see the connections more easily between different ideas and to better understand complex concepts. In a study conducted at the University of Santa Monica, it was found that entrainment at specific frequencies can enhance mathematical intelligence. After just eight weeks of practice, students who used entrainment showed significant improvements in their mathematical problem-solving ability compared to those who did not meditate with entrainment. The students who meditated also reported feeling more confident in their ability to handle mathematical problems.

Yinnergy can also be used to enhance logical intelligence. This type of intelligence is concerned with the ability to think critically and to see the connections between different ideas. By stilling the mind and achieving a greater state of clarity, individuals who listen to Yinnergy can more easily think abstractly, see the relationships between different ideas, and to draw logical conclusions.

Emotional Intelligence

Yinnergy is an effective way to enhance emotional intelligence, which is extremely helpful in managing our relationships. When we have a better understanding of our emotions, we can communicate them more effectively to others. We can also better understand the emotions of others, and how to respond to them in a way that is helpful and supportive. Yinnergy can help us to become more emotionally intelligent and to live a more fulfilling life.

Yinnergy can also help people become more compassionate and empathetic. The theory behind this is that by stimulating the brain stem (and the prefrontal cortex that is responsible for these types of feelings), they produce brain waves to become more attuned to the frequency of compassion and empathy. There is some anecdotal evidence that entrainment can indeed help people become more compassionate and empathetic, but more research is needed for verification.

Spatial Intelligence

This is the ability to think about things in three dimensions, which is a key part of spatial intelligence. By training your brain to focus in on the present, Yinnergy can help improve this type of intelligence by allowing you to see things more clearly, better understand the world around you, and see things from different perspectives.

When you meditate regularly, you will find that you become more aware of your surroundings and the details within them. Additionally, meditation can improve your memory by helping you to focus and retain information more effectively.

Lastly, the increased focus and problem-solving skills that you will develop through meditation can help you to improve this intelligence.

Musical Intelligence

Yinnergy is a form of entrainment program that can be used to improve musical intelligence. When we focus our attention on the present moment, we are better able to hear the subtle nuances in music and improve our ability to remember the melodies and harmonies we hear. This can help us to understand and memorize music better, and to become more proficient at playing an instrument.

Kinesthetic Intelligence

Yinnergy can help increase the ability to understand and respond to the sensations in one's body.

The practice of Yinnergy helps to develop a greater awareness of the body and how it moves. As a result of this increased awareness, practitioners of Yinnergy are better able to understand and respond to the sensations in their body. This can lead to improved coordination, balance, and proprioception.

Interpersonal Intelligence

Yinnergy has been shown to improve interpersonal intelligence by providing a space for people to connect with themselves on a deeper level. This self-awareness can then be transferred to interactions with others, allowing for greater understanding and communication. This can be beneficial in both personal and professional relationships, as it allows for more effective listening and interactions.

Intrapersonal Intelligence

Intrapersonal intelligence is defined as one's ability to understand oneself. This type of intelligence is important in achieving success in life, as it allows individuals to know their strengths and weaknesses, and to set realistic goals.

Yinnergy can improve intrapersonal intelligence by expanding self-awareness, increasing clarity of thought, and enhancing emotional stability. These benefits can all lead to improved intrapersonal intelligence.

Spiritual Intelligence

Yinnergy supports the development of positive qualities such as compassion, wisdom, and equanimity. Through the regular practice of entrainment, one can develop a deeper understanding of one's spiritual path which can lead to a greater sense of peace and contentment in life. In addition, this type of meditation can help to develop a stronger connection to the Divine.

Yinnergy also enhances spiritual intelligence by promoting a deeper understanding and connection to the inner self, and increasing our capacity for empathy and love. As we connect with our own inner peace and wisdom, we become more able to see the goodness in others and to offer them our compassion and support. We become more aware of the interconnectedness of all life, and our place within it.

Linguistic Intelligence

Linguistic intelligence is the capacity to use language to express what is on one's mind and to understand others. Linguistic intelligence allows people to communicate clearly and effectively, and to understand the nuances of language. Yinnergy has been shown to improve linguistic intelligence in several ways, by increasing awareness of the sounds of language, the meaning of words, the grammatical structure of language, and its cultural context.

All these things together help people to use language more effectively and to understand it more deeply. As a result, people who practice

Yinnergy meditation tend to be better and more effective communicators at the verbal and trans-verbal levels.

Naturalistic Intelligence

According to research, naturalistic intelligence is the ability to identify and classify natural objects and patterns. This intelligence enables one to effectively navigate and survive in the natural world. Furthermore, naturalistic intelligence has been linked to greater well-being and happiness. Meditation has been shown to improve naturalistic intelligence. A study published in *Frontiers in Psychology* found that participants who underwent eight weeks of meditation training showed significantly greater improvements in naturalistic intelligence than those in the control group. The study also found that the improvements in naturalistic intelligence were associated with increased self-reported well-being and happiness.

Yinnergy may improve naturalistic intelligence by increasing one's ability to focus and pay attention. Research has shown that naturalistic intelligence is associated with the ability to sustain attention and focus on tasks.

Yinnergy may also improve naturalistic intelligence by increasing one's ability to control emotions. Research has shown that naturalistic intelligence is associated with the ability to regulate emotions. This study found that participants showed increases in the ability to notice and understand patterns in nature. The study's lead author, Dr. Sara W. Lazar, said that the findings suggest that mindfulness meditation can help improve our ability to notice and understand patterns in nature. "This is an important ability because it helps us make better decisions about our environment, including everything from what to eat and where to live, to how to respond to climate change," she said. The findings suggest that mindfulness meditation may be a helpful tool for people who want to increase their naturalistic intelligence.

The Philosophy of Thinking

While there is still much to learn about the brain, we do know that the human brain has amazing capabilities. It is constantly active, constantly thinking, and constantly trying to make sense of the world around us. And all this thinking has a big impact on our mental and emotional health.

Critical Thinking

Meditation is an ancient practice that has been used for centuries to help people focus and find inner peace. In more recent years, meditation has been shown to have several benefits for critical thinking. A study published in the journal *Psychological Science* found that meditation can help improve cognitive flexibility, which is the ability to switch between different tasks or perspectives, as well as come up with creative solutions. The study showed that participants who underwent a four-week meditation program had better performance on a test of cognitive flexibility than those who did not meditate. And so, Yinnergy can help critical thinking by improving cognitive flexibility and increasing focus and attention (which allows people to process information more deeply and see different perspectives).

Transrational Thinking

Transrational thinking is beyond pre-rational and rational thinking. To advance as a human being in this context, transcending the rational is a must. So, to develop transrational thinking, one must first understand what these terms mean. Transrationality is defined as "beyond or transcending reason". In other words, transrationality is a higher form of thinking that is beyond the limitations of conventional reasoning.

The goal of Yinnergy is to quiet the mind and allow the practitioner to access a higher state of consciousness. In this state, the mind is free from bondage of the ego and the limitations of the rational mind. This allows the individual to think more clearly and creatively, and to access a higher level of intelligence.

Meta-Thinking

If there is such thing as transrational thinking, then what is meta-thinking? Meta-thinking is a natural by-product of transrationality. Meta-thinking is defined as "thinking about thinking". It is a reflective process of critically analyzing one's own thoughts and beliefs. When the mind is no longer bound by the ego and the limitations of rational thought, it is free to reflect on its own thoughts and beliefs. This process of self-reflection can lead to a greater understanding of oneself and the world around them.

Yinnergy can help develop meta-thinking by providing the individual with a tool to quiet the mind and access a deeper level of consciousness. This allows an individual to see beyond the linear thinking of the ego-mind and access a more creative and intuitive way of thinking.

The meta-thinking that can be developed through Yinnergy can help an individual to solve problems more creatively, make better decisions, and develop a more holistic view of the world.

Holistic Thinking

You have transrational thinking, meta-thinking, so what is next? Well, you also have holistic thinking, which is another lesser-known benefit of meditation. Holistic thinking is the ability to see the bigger picture and to understand how all the pieces fit together. It is a way of thinking that is both analytical and creative, taking into account both the parts and the whole.

Yinnergy is a powerful tool for developing holistic thinking. Just by listening to Yinnergy one hour a day, every day, allows you more access to the right hemisphere of the brain; it also allows you to quiet the mind and to focus on the present moment. This allows you to see things more clearly and to understand how they are connected. As you meditate, you will start to see how your thoughts, emotions, and actions are all interrelated. You will begin to see the interconnectedness of all things, and you will develop a more holistic view of the world.

Yinnergy can help you to develop holistic thinking in many areas of your life. For example, if you are trying to make a decision, Yinnergy can help you to see all the options and to understand how they will affect the whole.

Whole-Brain Thinking

Now this is where it gets very interesting. For these types of thinking to be at their best level of functioning, whole-brain synchronization must occur; and this is also called whole-brain thinking. Whole-brain thinking is a term used to describe the ability to use both sides of the brain to think and is often associated with creative and intuitive thinking. It is believed that when both sides of the brain are used to think, a person can come up with more creative solutions and ideas.

Whole-brain thinking is often said to be the key to success in many areas of life, such as business, art, and education. This is because it allows people to come up with more innovative and original ideas. There are many different techniques that can be used to develop whole-brain thinking and one of the most popular techniques, of course, is meditation. Meditation has been shown to be an effective way to improve this type of function, among many others.

Yinnergy is a type of meditation that is specifically designed to improve whole-brain thinking. This type of meditation synchronizes the two hemispheres of the brain, which allows for better communication between the two sides. This, in turn, leads to improved creativity, thinking, and problem solving. Whole-brain thinking and synchronization has also been linked to increased mental flexibility and higher levels of intelligence.

The journal *Frontiers in Psychology* published a study that found people who listened to binaural beats while working on a problem-solving task were more likely to find a creative solution than those who did not listen to binaural beats. Another study found that people who listened to binaural beats while working on a word-association task were better able to come up with creative responses than those who did not listen to binaural beats.

Thinking Without Thinking

Malcolm Gladwell's book *Blink* is all about the power of thinking without thinking. According to Gladwell, we often make better decisions when we go with our gut instinct rather than over-thinking things. Thinking without thinking is another benefit Yinnergy has to offer. This means that you can come up with solutions to problems more easily and make decisions more quickly; this is because, Yinnergy creates a bridge between the conscious and subconscious mind, which enhances the ability to think...by barely thinking about it.

Yinnergy and Creativity

The Power of Creativity

If you are hearing about brainwave entrainment for the first time, then you may not know that Yinnergy produces waveforms that encourage the brain to produce certain states. One of these states is known as the flow state, which is characterized by a deep sense of focus, concentration, and creativity. It is a state where ideas seem to flow effortlessly, and the individual can produce their best work.

Yinnergy has been shown to be effective in enhancing creativity in a variety of tasks, including problem solving, brainstorming, and writing. The mechanism by which Yinnergy enhances creativity is not fully understood, but it is thought to work by producing brainwave patterns that are conducive to flow states. While in the flow state, the individual is in a heightened state of awareness, and can access more of their brain's potential. This results in improved focus, concentration, and creativity.

Yinnergy is a safe and effective way to improve creativity. It is a non-invasive form of brainwave entrainment that uses audio tones to encourage the brain to produce specific brainwaves. When used correctly, Yinnergy can help the brain to produce more alpha and theta waves, which are associated with enhanced creative thinking.

Innovation

Yinnergy can support innovation in the following ways:
- **Accessing Higher Levels of Consciousness:** One of the main ways in which Yinnergy can support innovation is by helping individuals to access higher levels of consciousness and creativity by stimulating the prefrontal cortex and the thalamus. This can be achieved by using specific frequencies and sound patterns.
- **Increasing Levels of Focus and Concentration:** Strengthening the prefrontal cortex can also help to increase levels of focus and concentration. This can be beneficial for those who are working on innovative projects to help maintain their focus and concentration for longer periods of time.

- **Supporting Team Collaboration:** Yinnergy can also be used to support collaboration and reduce conflict within teams. This is because the increased levels of communication and understanding that are achieved during Yinnergy can help team members to work together more effectively.
- **Improving Decision Making:** Stimulating the prefrontal cortex can also help to improve decision making because the increased levels of communication and understanding that are achieved during Yinnergy can help people share information and reach consensus more quickly.
- **Supporting Change:** Yinnergy can also help support change by stimulating the amygdala, which is responsible for processing emotions related to anxiety and fear. This can help people to accept and implement change more easily.

Flow States

Flow states are a mental state where we feel completely absorbed and focused in the present moment. We become so engrossed in what we are doing that all sense of time and self disappears. When we are in this state of complete concentration, our performance becomes effortless.

Flow states have been studied in a variety of fields including sports, the arts, and business. Researchers have found that flow state experiences lead to peak performance and increased creativity. For those of you who are intrigued by this and would like to attain this, a flow state can be reached through deliberate practice and deep concentration; and once you reach a flow state, you are able to achieve things you never thought possible. Yinnergy can produce flow states by training the mind to become more focused and present.

Yinnergy can help to quiet the mind chatter that keeps us from being fully engaged in the moment. As we become more proficient in the practice, we can enter deeper states of meditation where we become more aware of the present moment and less attached to thoughts and emotions. This can lead to a sense of calm and peace.

Yinnergy and Brain Health

The Brain and its Function

Some people are naturally gifted with great intelligence and creativity. However, for most people, these abilities can be enhanced with the help of Yinnergy.

Yinnergy increases brain function in a variety of ways, including:
- Increasing blood flow and oxygen to the brain
- Increasing the production of neurotransmitters
- Increasing brainwave activity
- Increasing the number of brain cells
- Enhancing the function of existing brain cells
- Enhancing overall brain function

All of these effects work together to improve brain function, which can lead to greater creativity, genius-level thinking, and improved performance in a variety of areas.

Facets of the Brain

As we now know, meditation is an effective way to stimulate the brain. It has been shown to increase the activity of the brain stem, the limbic system (the hippocampus, the thalamus, and the amygdala), the auditory cortex (the part of the brain responsible for processing), the reticular formation, and the prefrontal cortex.

The Brain Stem

The brain stem is the lowermost portion of the brain that connects the cerebral cortex with the spinal cord. It is responsible for basic life-sustaining functions, such as heart rate, breathing, and blood pressure. Some research suggests that meditation may help to improve the function of the brain stem, as well as the overall health of the brain. Additionally, meditation has been shown to reduce stress and anxiety, which can also impact the brain stem.

The Reticular Formation

The reticular formation is a network of interconnected neurons that extends throughout the brain stem. It plays an important role in attention, arousal, and sleep. Meditation has been shown to increase activity in the reticular formation, which can lead to improved focus and concentration.

The Pineal Gland

The pineal gland is a small gland in the brain that is responsible for the production of melatonin. Melatonin is a hormone that helps regulate the sleep-wake cycle. It is generally believed that meditation can help to activate the pineal gland and produce beneficial changes in brain wave activity. Additionally, meditation has been shown to reduce stress and improve overall well-being, which may also lead to improved pineal gland function.

The Limbic System

The limbic system is a set of structures in the brain that are involved in emotion, motivation, and memory. These structures include the amygdala, hippocampus, and thalamus. The limbic system is important for survival-related behaviors, such as eating and drinking. It also plays a role in emotional responses, such as fear and aggression, and helping the brain form new memories. Some research has suggested that meditation can help to regulate the limbic system.

The Amygdala

The amygdala is the part of the brain that is responsible for the fight-or-flight response. When someone is meditating, they are typically in a relaxed state, which means that the amygdala is not activated.

The Hippocampus

The hippocampus is a small, seahorse-shaped structure that is located within the brain's medial temporal lobe. This region of the brain is important for learning, and the formation and retrieval of memories. The hippocampus is believed to play a role in spatial memory, which is our ability to remember where things are located in our environment. The hippocampus is also thought to be involved in navigational tasks, such as finding our way around a new city. Meditation has been found to increase the size of the hippocampus.

The Thalamus

The thalamus is responsible for processing and relaying sensory information to the brain. Meditation has been shown to affect the thalamus by reducing the amount of sensory information that it processes. This can lead to a decrease in the amount of stress and anxiety that a person feels.

The Auditory Cortex

The auditory cortex is the part of the brain that processes sound, is responsible for identifying and interpreting them, and for helping to regulate the body's response to them. Some research suggests that meditation may lead to changes in the way the brain processes sound. For example, one study published in the journal *Frontiers in Human Neuroscience* in 2012 found that individuals who regularly practiced meditation had increased activity in brain regions associated with attention and decreased activity in regions associated with mind-wandering, which may lead to better ability to ignore irrelevant sounds and focus on relevant ones. Additionally, another study published in the journal *Psychological Science* in 2014 found that mindfulness meditation training improved the ability of participants to sustain attention and inhibit mind-wandering, which may also support the idea that meditation practices can enhance focus.

The Prefrontal Cortex

The prefrontal cortex is the area of the brain that controls executive function, which includes planning, decision making, and working memory. This area of the brain is also responsible for regulating emotions. Some potential effects of meditation on the prefrontal cortex include increased focus and concentration, improved self-awareness, and enhanced emotional regulation. Yinnergy helps to improve these effects by providing a more stable and harmonious environment for the brain to function in by synchronizing the left and right hemispheres of the brain. This synchronization helps the brain function

The Default Mode Network

The default mode network (DMN) is a set of interconnected brain regions that are active when a person is not focused on the outside world or engaged in a task. These regions are involved in a variety of functions, including self-reflection, daydreaming, and memory consolidation. Meditation affects the default mode network by reducing the amount of time that people spend in that default mode. Yinnergy also deactivates the default mode network within the brain. This network is thought to be responsible for a person's self-awareness and introspection. When the DMN is active, a person is more likely to be thinking about themselves and their thoughts and feelings. However, when the DMN is deactivated, a person is more likely to be focused on the present moment and their surroundings. This is why Yinnergy is beneficial for a person's mental health. It can help to focus a person's thoughts and attention on the present moment, rather than on their internal thoughts and feelings.

The Posterior Cingulate Cortex

The posterior cingulate cortex is responsible for higher-order cognitive functions such as attention, language, and memory. Yinnergy stimulates the posterior cingulate cortex by producing a third neutral tone when the left and right hemispheres of the brain are synced. Yinnergy may be able to improve these cognitive functions in both healthy individuals and those with dementia.

Neurons, Dendrites, and Synapses

Neurons are the basic units of the nervous system and are responsible for transmitting information throughout the body. There are three main types of neurons: sensory neurons, motor neurons, and interneurons. Sensory neurons are responsible for detecting changes in the environment and relaying that information to the brain. Motor neurons are responsible for controlling muscle movement. Interneurons are responsible for connecting different parts of the nervous system.

Neurons are made up of a cell body, an axon, and dendrites. The cell body contains the nucleus, which houses the DNA. The axon is a long, thin fiber that transmits information from the cell body to the dendrites. And the dendrites are short, branching fibers that receive information from other neurons.

Neurons communicate with each other through electrical and chemical signals. Electrical signals are produced by the movement of ions across the cell membrane. Chemical signals are produced by the release of neurotransmitters.

Neurons are constantly changing in response to the environment. They can change their structure, their function, and even their location in the body.

Researchers have found that the synchronization of brainwaves alters the structure of neurons in the prefrontal cortex. This alteration in neurons is believed to be responsible for the brain entrainment benefits for depression and anxiety, cognition, and creativity.

Dendrites are the branch-like extensions of neurons that develop new connections when you learn skills or form memories. Dendrites are responsible for receiving electrochemical signals and transmitting them to the neuron for further processing. When your dendrites grow, your ability to learn new things increases, and you can create stronger and more long-lasting memories. Dendrites are important for healthy brain function because they receive messages from other neurons. They are like the "branches" on a tree that receive water and nutrients from the roots and "transmit" them to the rest of the tree. Neurons communicate with each other by sending electrochemical signals across synapses. Dendrites are the projections of neurons that intercept incoming signals. They act like "antennae" that pick up the transmissions from neighboring neurons and convey them to the rest of the neural network.

When you meditate with Yinnergy or do any other activity that entrains your brain, it produces chemicals and electromagnetic frequencies that help in the growth of new dendrites and synapses. This supports the growth of new dendrites and stronger connections between neurons. Increased dendrite growth is associated with improved cognition and better memory.

Synapses are the tiny spaces between neurons (brain cells), where signals pass from one neuron to another. If we think about these signals as waves, the synapses act like a bridge between the two neurons, allowing the signal to pass between them. They are made up of two parts: the presynaptic terminal and the postsynaptic terminal. The presynaptic terminal of one neuron is connected to the postsynaptic terminal of another. Synapses are crucial for proper brain function. They are responsible for transmitting and receiving signals between neurons, as well as controlling the strength of those signals. They can be likened to the strength of a connection between two people; some people are good at keeping in touch, while others only call when they need something. This is the same for neurons; some are strong, and others have a weaker relationship that could end at any time.

When you listen to Yinnergy, certain effects will be highly pronounced, like a pulsing sound or a rhythm that you can feel. Whenever you hear this, your brain will try to match it by producing a similar effect to make sense of it. In this case, it will try to produce a rhythmic signal or electrical pulse itself. This is why brain entrainment affects the synapses in the brain; it is causing them to produce these effects naturally.

There are three primary ways in which Yinnergy affects the synapses in the brain and improves their function:

Synaptic Gaps

As mentioned, synaptic gaps are the tiny spaces between neurons, where signals pass from one neuron to another. Yinnergy affects the synapses in the brain by increasing the gap between them, making it easier for the signals to pass through. This is super helpful for people who have a lot of pressure on their brains and find it hard to focus. As the gap between neurons increases, there is less pressure on the brain, making it easier to focus.

Synaptic Strength

Yinnergy affects the synapses in the brain by making the signals between neurons stronger. This is helpful for people who find it hard to concentrate or have a short attention span. A stronger signal between neurons makes it easier to stay on task and ignore distractions.

Synaptic Formation

The third effect of Yinnergy is the formation of new synapses in the brain. This is super helpful for people who want to learn a new skill or expand their knowledge base. New synapses mean new connections between neurons, which means you can learn things much more easily. This is incredibly helpful for students or people who want to improve their mental capabilities.

Microtubules

Microtubules are small, tubular structures that are found in the cells of eukaryotes (a domain of living organisms whose cells have a nucleus). They are made up of the protein tubulin and are important in a variety of cellular processes, including cell division, cell motility, and cell structure. Microtubules are also involved in transporting materials within cells. Yinnergy may be able to change the structure of microtubules, and this could affect how cells function.

The Relationship Between Microtubules and Consciousness

The theory that consciousness is in the microtubules was first proposed by neuroscientist, Roger Penrose, and anesthesiologist, Stuart Hameroff. They suggested that the quantum information processing that takes place in the microtubules could be the seat of consciousness. This theory is still being explored and debated by scientists today. Microtubules are one of the most important components of cells, and if the theory is correct, they are also essential for consciousness. Microtubules are responsible for organizing and structuring the cells of the body, and they also play a role in communication between cells. There is evidence that microtubules are involved in consciousness in two ways.

First, microtubules are necessary for the proper functioning of the brain's electrical system. Second, microtubules may be responsible for the storage and retrieval of memories. Without microtubules, cells would be unable to communicate with each other, and the brain would be unable to function properly. This suggests that microtubules are necessary for consciousness. The deeper levels of Yinnergy may affect microtubules because of its lower carrier-frequencies and infrasound waves, which makes this a very powerful technology.

Quantum vibration is an important aspect of microtubule function. It is the basic motion of all particles at the atomic and subatomic levels. It is the smallest possible unit of motion and is the building block of all larger motions. All matter is made up of vibrating particles, and the properties of matter are determined by the frequency and amplitude of these vibrations.

By understanding how microtubules vibrate, we can better understand how they carry out their important functions within cells. Microtubules are made up of tubulin proteins that self-assemble into long, hollow cylinders. These tubulin proteins can vibrate at high frequencies, and it is these vibrations that allow microtubules to perform their various functions.

One important function of microtubules is to act as a scaffold for the cell by organizing other proteins and molecules within the cell. This organization is important for many cellular processes, including cell division. Microtubules can also act as highways for proteins and other molecules to travel around the cell. This is possible because microtubules can rapidly change their shape and their tubulin proteins can vibrate at very high frequencies.

For microtubules to carry out these functions, they need to be able to communicate with each other. This communication is made possible by the quantum vibrations of the tubulin proteins, which allow microtubules to communicate with each other through a process called quantum entanglement. Quantum entanglement is a physical phenomenon that occurs when pairs or groups of particles are generated, interact, or share spatial proximity in ways such that the quantum state of each particle cannot be described independently of the state of the others, even when the particles are separated by a large distance—instead, a quantum state must be described for the system as a whole.

The Power of Infrasound and its Effect on Microtubules

The thirteenth level of Yinnergy uses pitch frequencies within the infrasound range to create the entrainment, which is below 20 Hz. Infrasound is a sound that is lower in frequency than what humans can hear. The human ear cannot hear it, but it can be felt. Infrasound can be produced naturally by earthquakes, volcanoes, and ocean waves. It is often used in studies of animal communication, as many animals can hear infrasound. Infrasound can also be produced by man-made sources such as wind turbines and engines. It can travel long distances and can be used to detect and locate objects.

Infrasound has been used for centuries by the ancient Egyptians and Mayans. It is said that infrasound can cause a feeling of awe, and even fear, which plays a huge role in peak spiritual experiences. Infrasound can travel long distances and can even penetrate other objects, including the skull. Infrasound has been used in many studies to induce altered states of consciousness, as well as sleep, meditation, and out-of-body experiences.

Infrasound has also been shown to have physical effects on the body. Infrasound at these lower levels is used for entrainment. The tone creates vibrations in the air or through headphones that the brain can interpret as sound. These vibrations can travel through the skull, or through the inner ear, where they stimulate the auditory nerve. The auditory nerve sends signals to the brain, using these vibrations to create the entrainment.

Infrasound vibrates at frequencies that are below the human threshold for hearing, although it may also be below the human threshold for comprehension. EEG patterns are thought to be influenced by this frequency, leading to even deeper states of altered consciousness.

It is believed by some experts that infrasound can affect microtubules. Studies have been conducted where cells were exposed to infrasound at different frequencies for different periods of time. The results showed that infrasound caused changes in the structure of microtubules, including how they were arranged and how they interacted with other proteins. These changes in microtubule structure could have several consequences for the cell, such as the way that cells divide or communicate with each other. Additionally, these changes could have an impact on the function of microtubules. Infrasound has been shown to cause changes in the brain waves of people exposed to it and may affect what we perceive as consciousness.

While it is not well understood how infrasound may affect molecules, it may influence them by causing the molecules to vibrate. This vibration could potentially disrupt their structure by breaking them down and causing them to restructure at higher levels of development.

Infrasound can also affect atoms. Atoms are constantly in motion, and they vibrate at a certain frequency. When they are exposed to infrasound, their vibration frequency can change. This can alter the atoms' structure and properties, which can have a ripple effect on the molecules that they are a part of. In turn, this can change the physical and chemical properties of the material that the molecules are a part of.

Infrasound may also affect subatomic particles by causing them to vibrate at a higher frequency. This could lead to a change in the way they interact with each other and with their surroundings. Additionally, it is possible that infrasound could cause particles to become excited or emit energy.

Some people believe that infrasound may also affect the fabric of reality itself. This is based on the idea of "branes" in string theory. The string theory framework posits that there are multiple dimensions beyond our own four. These extra dimensions are compactified, or rolled up, into very small sizes. Our four dimensions are said to be like a membrane, or "brane", floating in this higher-dimensional space. Some theories suggest that infrasound may cause vibrations in these extra dimensions, which could then be felt as effects in our own four dimensions. This could explain some of the strange effects that have been reported with infrasound, such as ghost sightings and poltergeist activity. It is also possible that infrasound could be used to manipulate these extra dimensions in some way, although this is purely speculative at this point.

Neural Melanin

Neural melanin is a pigment that is found in the central nervous system. It is thought to play a role in the development and function of the nervous system.

It is believed that meditation may be beneficial to neural melanin in the brain. The pigment that is responsible for the dark color of the brain. This is significant because neural melanin is known to play a role in cognitive function and memory.

Neural melanin is found in high concentrations in the substantia nigra, a small, black, almond-shaped structure located in the midbrain that is involved with several important functions, including movement control, balance, and coordination. The substantia nigra also plays a role in reward-seeking behavior and addiction.

The substantia nigra is made up of two parts: the pars compacta and the pars reticulata. The pars compacta is the main region responsible for producing dopamine, a neurotransmitter that is essential for motor function. The pars reticulata is responsible for processing information from the pars compacta and sending it to the thalamus.

Brain Receptors

A brain receptor is a protein found on the surface of a brain cell that helps to regulate the activities of that cell. There are many different types of brain receptors, each with a different function, including receiving chemical or electrical signals from other cells, mediating the effects of neurotransmitters, or processing the sense of touch, taste, or smell. It is a well-known fact that meditation can positively influence the brain. However, what is not as well-known is that meditation can also influence brain receptors.

There are two main types of brain receptors: excitatory and inhibitory. Excitatory receptors are responsible for increasing neural activity, while inhibitory receptors are responsible for decreasing it. When it comes to meditation, the practice can help to increase the activity of inhibitory receptors. Inhibitory receptors are important because they help to control the level of neural activity. Too much neural activity can lead to problems such as anxiety, while too little neural activity can lead to problems such as depression. Therefore, by increasing the activity of inhibitory receptors, meditation can help to regulate the level of neural activity, and consequently, improve mental health. There is still much research to be done in this area, but the current evidence suggests that meditation can indeed positively influence brain receptors.

Meditation has been shown to increase the activity of the GABA receptors, leading to a decrease in anxiety and stress. Meditation has also been shown to increase the activity of serotonin receptors, which increases mood and decreases depression.

The Olivary Nucleus

The olivary nucleus is a small, round structure located in the medulla oblongata, just dorsal to the inferior olivary nucleus. It is one of the three nuclei that make up the reticular formation of the medulla oblongata.

The olivary nucleus is the largest of the three nuclei and is divided into two parts: the medial olivary nucleus and the lateral olivary nucleus.

The medial olivary nucleus is larger than the lateral olivary nucleus and is divided into three parts: the dorsal, ventral, and medial nuclei. The dorsal and ventral nuclei are further divided into three subnuclei: the rostral, caudal, and central subnuclei.

The olivary nucleus receives input from the contralateral cerebral hemisphere via the medial lemniscus. This input is then relayed to the contralateral inferior olivary nucleus. The olivary nucleus also receives input from the ipsilateral inferior olivary nucleus and the ipsilateral pontine nuclei.

The olivary nucleus is important for the transmission of motor commands from the brain stem to the spinal cord. It is also involved in the processing of auditory and visual information, and responsible for the production of electrical impulses that travel down the spinal cord and stimulate the muscles to contract.

The olivary nucleus is stimulated by the neurotransmitter acetylcholine. Acetylcholine is released from the motor neurons of the olivary nucleus and binds to the receptors on the cell surface of the target muscle. This triggers a muscle contraction.

The olivary nucleus is also responsible for the regulation of blood pressure and heart rate. It does this by sending impulses to the vasomotor center in the medulla oblongata, which in turn regulates the diameter of the blood vessels.

Yinnergy influences the olivary nucleus by causing it to produce electrical impulses at a lower frequency than the impulses it normally produces. This has the effect of slowing down the activity of the olivary nucleus, which has been shown to have positive effects on the brain and body including improved mood, decreased anxiety, improved sleep, increased focus and concentration, increased feelings of well-being and relaxation, reduced symptoms of depression, reduced symptoms of PTSD, and reduced symptoms of ADHD. Additionally, this type of stimulation has been shown to help improve cognitive function and memory.

Low Carrier Frequencies for Evolution

When you listen to any Yinnergy soundtrack, the low carrier frequencies embedded within the beat frequencies push your brain to greater levels of complexity, stimulating it so that it functions more efficiently and processes more information. This allows you to reach higher states of consciousness, where you can perceive reality with broader awareness and more perspectives. You will no longer be limited by your point of view. Instead, you will be able to understand and empathize with others, even if they have different points of view. The more you use Yinnergy, the higher your state of consciousness will become. As we move into higher states of consciousness, we open ourselves up to a broader sense of awareness and begin to see reality from multiple perspectives. This expanded awareness can bring several benefits, including a greater sense of understanding and empathy for others, a deeper connection to our inner wisdom, and a greater ability to manifest our desires.

When we perceive reality this way, we can see the interconnectedness of all things and how our actions impact the world around us. We also begin to see that there is more to life than what we can see and touch in the physical world. We may start to feel a connection to a higher power or to the energy that flows through all things.

This expanded awareness can lead to a greater sense of peace and well-being, as well as a deeper understanding of our purpose in life.

Yinnergy also helps to push your nervous system to more complexity. This helps your body handle more stress and anxiety, allowing you to live a more peaceful and stress-free life.

If you want to reach the highest levels of consciousness, it is important to commit to using Yinnergy regularly. Brainwave entrainment with low carrier frequency sound waves stimulate specific parts of the brain. This results in the brain and nervous system being pushed to restructure themselves and evolve to higher levels of development, because the low-frequency sound stimulates the growth and repair of nerve cells, as well as the formation of new connections between them. In other words, low carrier frequencies help the brain to grow and develop healthily, leading to improved function and overall mental health. By improving communication between different parts of the brain, low carrier frequencies can help to increase our focus and concentration. It can also help to improve our memory and to process information more effectively. It can also help to release any built-up tension or stress. When our brain is more relaxed, it is better able to focus on tasks and learn new information.

This process is based on the principle of entrainment, which states that when two or more objects vibrate at the same frequency, they will become synchronized. In the case of low carrier frequencies, the sound waves stimulate the brain, causing it to vibrate at the same, or close, to those frequencies. This synchronization of brainwaves leads to several benefits, including improved mental clarity, increased focus and concentration, and enhanced relaxation.

When our brainwaves are in a slow frequency range (such as delta or theta states), combined with low carrier frequencies (which create a higher amplitude), our brain is more open to change. This is because these low carrier frequencies allow for more communication between different parts of the brain. When our brain is more open to change, it is more likely to restructure itself and evolve to higher levels of complexity, changing how we see the world.

Low carrier frequencies in the delta range cause the limbic system to release repressed unconscious material. This release can be beneficial for those who suffer from trauma or PTSD. The release of repressed material can also help to improve mood and reduce anxiety and depression. The limbic system is responsible for regulating emotions, and when it is not functioning properly, it can lead to emotional distress. By stimulating the limbic system with low carrier frequency binaural beats, it is possible to release repressed emotions and help the individual to feel better.

Overall, low carrier frequencies are a powerful tool to improve our brain function (including whole brain thinking) and our overall health in a safe and non-invasive way.

Another powerful benefit of low carrier frequencies is that they are the equivalent of a longer meditation session (which is well-known among advanced meditators). It is widely accepted that the key to a successful meditation practice is consistency. The more frequently you meditate, the deeper your practice will become and the more benefits you will experience. However, for many people, finding the time to meditate for even just a few minutes each day can be a challenge. This is where low carrier frequencies can be extremely helpful, as by meditating with them, you are effectively lengthening your meditation session. This is because these frequencies create a deep state of relaxation and stillness in the mind, similar to the state achieved after years of meditation practice. In other words, by meditating with low carrier frequencies, you can achieve the benefits of a long meditation session in a much shorter period.

To be clear, the lower the carrier frequency, the more time it is the equivalent time spent in a traditional meditation session. For example, in traditional meditation, one would have to meditate three hours a day every day for 20.8 years to reach

50,000 hours. But with Yinnergy, one would only have to spend one hour a day for 62.5 days to reach the equivalent of 50, 000 hours.

The acceleration of progress with meditation practice using Yinnergy cultivates the possibility of achieving a state of enlightenment, whether suddenly or gradually. Sudden enlightenment is a direct and immediate understanding of the true nature of reality, while gradual enlightenment is a more incremental understanding that occurs over time. Both are valid approaches to understanding the nature of reality, but which one is more beneficial depends on the individual.

Some people may prefer sudden enlightenment because it is a more deep, direct, and immediate understanding of reality, and they want to live by that understanding. Others may prefer gradual enlightenment because it allows them to slowly integrate the understanding of reality into their lives and make changes gradually.

Which approach is more beneficial ultimately depends on the individual and what they are seeking to gain from the understanding of reality, but both approaches are possible through the deeper levels of the Yinnergy program, and with long-term practice.

Additionally, Yinnergy is a powerful tool that can be used to heighten your senses and perception.

When used correctly, it can lead to some amazing and life-changing experiences.

Some of the most common Yinnergy heightening phenomena include feeling as if the physical body has split in half during meditation; encountering a bright light during meditation; natural highs and intoxication; moments of bliss, love, vivid dreams; and full-body orgasms lasting for hours.

Additionally, the use of Yinnergy can temporarily help to heighten psychic phenomenon by synchronizing the brainwave patterns of the user. This can help to create a more focused and clear state of mind, which can be conducive to experiencing greater psychic abilities.

Some people who have used Yinnergy reported experiencing increased psychic abilities, such as being able to see into the future or reading other people's thoughts. Other users have reported having visions, lucid dreams, and out-of-body experiences. There is no scientific evidence to support these claims. However, many people believe that it works.

While these experiences may not happen for everyone, they can be extremely intense and overwhelming, but they are also incredibly beautiful and life-affirming.

Neurotransmitters and Hormones

Ever wondered why you feel the way you do? This has to do with neurochemicals called neurotransmitters. For example, love is one of the most powerful emotions we experience as human beings. It can make us feel happy, sad, anxious, and everything in between. Love is also a complex chemical process that happens in our brains, which is the combination of dopamine, serotonin, oxytocin, and vasopressin. When we fall in love, certain neurotransmitters are released that cause us to feel elated, happy, and connected to the object of our affection.

Yinnergy is an effective way to release and regulate these neurotransmitters within the brain. When we meditate, we activate the areas of the brain associated with pleasure and happiness. This increases the levels of these chemicals in our brain, which leads to feelings of relaxation and well-being. We can also eventually let go of any intrusive thoughts, which helps to calm the mind.

Neurotransmitters are chemicals that transmit signals in the nervous system. They are released from neurons (nerve cells) and bind to receptors on other neurons. This binding process triggers a change in the receiving neuron, which then transmits the signal. There are many different types of neurotransmitters, each with different functions. Some of the more important neurotransmitters for mental health include serotonin, dopamine, and gamma-aminobutyric acid (GABA).

Serotonin

Serotonin is involved in mood regulation, appetite, and sleep. A deficiency in serotonin has been linked to depression, anxiety, and other mental health disorders. Meditation has been shown to increase serotonin levels. In one study, "Meditation experience is associated with increased cortical thickness" published in *NeuroReport* in 2005, people who meditated for eight weeks had increased levels of serotonin and felt happier and more content than those who did not meditate. Meditation can also help to regulate sleep and appetite, two other functions that serotonin is responsible for. Therefore, meditation can have a positive impact on mental health by increasing serotonin levels.

Dopamine

Dopamine is involved in motivation, reward, and pleasure. A deficiency in dopamine has been linked to attention deficit hyperactivity disorder (ADHD), addiction, and other mental health disorders. Meditation has been shown to increase dopamine levels in the brain. One such study, published in the journal *Proceedings of the National Academy of Sciences* in 2011, found that participants who practiced mindfulness meditation for 12 hours over 4 days had increased dopamine levels and improved cognitive flexibility. Other research has shown that meditation can help to reduce stress and anxiety, which can also lead to increased dopamine levels.

GABA

GABA is involved in anxiety and stress relief. A deficiency in GABA has been linked to anxiety, depression, and other mental health disorders. Meditation has been shown to be beneficial in releasing these neurotransmitters. According to a study published in *Frontiers in Neuroscience*, meditation increased levels of GABA, which led to a reduction in anxiety.

Oxytocin

Oxytocin is a hormone that is produced by the hypothalamus in the brain. It is best known for its role in promoting bonding and maternal behavior. Oxytocin is also involved in other important functions, such as regulating stress and anxiety, and promoting social behavior and communication. Meditation has been shown to increase oxytocin levels in the brain. There have been several studies that investigated the effects of mindfulness meditation on oxytocin levels and prosocial behavior. For example, a study published in the *Frontiers in Human Neuroscience* in 2016 found that an 8-week mindfulness-based stress-reduction program was associated with increased oxytocin levels and improved social cognition in individuals with social anxiety disorder. Another study published in the *Journal of Positive Psychology* in 2015 found that a 4-week mindfulness intervention was associated with increased prosocial behavior and positive affect, and these effects were mediated by increased oxytocin levels.

Vasopressin

Vasopressin is a hormone that helps regulate the body's water balance. It is released by the pituitary gland in response to changes in blood pressure or blood volume. Vasopressin acts on the kidneys to conserve water and increase blood pressure. It also has a role in regulating blood sugar levels. Meditation has been shown to have a positive effect on vasopressin levels. In studies, it has been found that meditation may have an effect on vasopressin levels. For example, a study published in the journal *Psychoneuroendocrinology* in 2016 found that an 8-week mindfulness-based stress-reduction program was associated with decreased vasopressin levels in women with post-traumatic stress disorder. Another study published in the *International Journal of Behavioral Medicine* in 2014, found that a 12-week mindfulness-based stress-reduction program, participants had significant reductions in vasopressin levels and cortisol levels, and these changes were associated with improvements in perceived stress and emotional regulation.

The participants who meditated also had lower blood pressure and heart rate, and they reported feeling less stressed. There are several possible explanations for how meditation lowers vasopressin levels. One theory is that meditation decreases the activity of the sympathetic nervous system, which is responsible for the fight-or-flight response. This can lead to a decrease in blood pressure and heart rate. Whatever the mechanism, the results of this study suggest that meditation can have a positive effect on vasopressin levels and may help to reduce stress and promote relaxation.

The role of oxytocin and vasopressin in love has been widely studied. Oxytocin is sometimes called the "cuddle hormone" because it is released when people hug or touch. Vasopressin is involved in pair bonding and increases the feeling of attachment. Both hormones are released during sex and can help create a bond between partners. Oxytocin is also released when a mother bonds with her baby. It helps with trust and attachment. There is some evidence that oxytocin and vasopressin play a role in social anxiety and autism. People with these conditions have trouble reading social cues and may not bond as easily with others. Studies have shown that oxytocin can increase empathy. It may also help with bonding, trust, and attachment.

Nutrition for Brain and Gut Health

Supplements

A diet rich in healthy fats, antioxidants, vitamins, and minerals is essential for brain health. These nutrients protect the brain from damage, support cognitive function, and promote healthy brain development.

Fatty acids are a major component of cell membranes and are essential for proper cell function. The brain is composed of 60% fat and needs a constant supply of healthy fats to function properly. Omega-3 fatty acids are particularly important for brain health, as they support cognitive function and protect the brain from damage.

Antioxidants help to protect the brain from damage caused by free radicals. Free radicals are unstable molecules that can damage cells and lead to inflammation.

Vitamin C, vitamin E, and beta-carotene are all powerful antioxidants that can help to protect the brain. Vitamins and minerals are essential for many biochemical reactions in the body and are necessary for proper brain function.

Vitamins B6, B12, and folic acid are important for the synthesis of neurotransmitters, which are essential for brain function.

Magnesium is a mineral that is involved in over 300 biochemical reactions in the body. This mineral is essential for proper nerve and muscle function, and studies have shown that it can help to improve mood and reduce anxiety.

Iron and calcium are all essential for healthy brain development.

Foods and Gut Health

A nutritious diet is important for maintaining a healthy brain and nervous system.

Omega-3 fatty acids can be found in flaxseeds and chia seeds. B vitamins are found in whole grains, dark leafy greens, nuts, and seeds. Antioxidants are found in colorful fruits and vegetables, such as blueberries, strawberries, and kale.

Incorporating these nutritious foods into your diet is a great way to support a healthy brain and nervous system.

Sessions of Yinnergy can be enhanced by paying

attention to the quality of the foods we eat and the supplements we take. Just as the body needs the right fuel to function optimally, the mind also benefits from nourishment.

When we eat whole, nutrient-rich foods, we are providing our bodies with the building blocks it needs to function properly. This includes the brain, which needs certain nutrients to function optimally.

The Gut

The human gut is often referred to as the "second brain." This is because the gut is home to a large number of neurons, which are responsible for many of the body's functions. The gut is also responsible for producing many of the body's hormones and neurotransmitters.

There is a strong belief in the gut-brain connection in Taoism, and it is thought that a healthy gut is essential for a healthy mind. Taoists believe that by keeping the gut healthy, we can keep the mind healthy and vice versa.

The gut-brain connection is a two-way street. The brain can influence the gut, and the gut can influence the brain. For example, the brain can send signals to the gut that influence appetite and digestion. And the gut can send signals to the brain that influence mood and behavior. The brain-gut connection is a complex one, and scientists are still trying to understand how the two are connected.

There is a growing body of evidence that suggests that the gut-brain connection is a major factor in many diseases and disorders, including obesity, diabetes, heart disease, and depression. So, if you want to keep your brain healthy, it is important to take care of your gut.

Eating a healthy diet, exercising regularly, and managing stress can all help keep your gut-brain connection strong.

The brain and the gut are connected through the vagus nerve, which is the longest nerve in the body. The vagus nerve starts in the brain stem and goes all the way down to the stomach. This connection allows the brain to send signals to the gut, and the gut to send signals to the brain.

The vagus nerve is responsible for many functions, including heart rate, digestion, and immunity. The connection between the gut and the brain is complex and bidirectional. The gut can influence the brain through the nervous system and the release of hormones.

The brain and the gut are connected because of their role in digestion. The brain controls the muscles that move food through the digestive system. The gut also helps to break down food so that the nutrients can be absorbed into the bloodstream.

The gut-brain connection is important for maintaining a healthy digestive system. When the brain and the gut are not working together properly, it can lead to problems such as constipation, diarrhea, and irritable bowel syndrome.

The vagus nerve is not the only connection between the brain and the gut. Some hormones are released by the gut that can affect the brain. For example, serotonin is a hormone that is involved in regulating mood and appetite. It is produced in the gut and then sent to the brain where it can influence mood.

Problems with the brain-gut connection have been linked to several mental health disorders, such as anxiety, depression, and even autism.

However, there are key ways in which the brain and gut communicate with each other. One way is through the nervous system (made up of the brain, the spinal cord, and every nerve in the body). The nervous system is responsible for sending messages back and forth between the brain and the rest of the body.

The gut has its own nervous system, called the enteric nervous system, which is made up of a network of neurons in the gut. This enteric nervous system is in constant communication with the brain through the nervous system. The enteric nervous system (ENS) is a network of nerves that runs from the esophagus to the rectum and is responsible for the motility of the GI tract. The ENS is sometimes referred to as the "brain in the gut" because it can communicate with the brain via the vagus nerve.

The gut also communicates with the brain through the release of hormones. Hormones are chemicals that are produced by endocrine cells and released into the bloodstream, where they travel to various organs to regulate their function. For example, the hormone insulin is produced by the pancreas and regulates blood sugar levels. The hormone ghrelin is produced by the stomach and increases appetite.

Yinnergy is an effective way to improve gut health. A study published in the *Journal of Gastrointestinal and Liver Diseases* in 2016 found that a mindfulness-based stress-reduction program led to significant improvements in symptoms of irritable bowel syndrome (IBS) including abdominal pain and bowel habits in a group of adults with IBS. Similarly, another study conducted in 2017, published in *Journal of Clinical Diagnosis and Research*, found that a combination of yoga and meditation was effective in reducing IBS symptoms in a group of women. These studies suggest that meditation may be a beneficial complementary treatment for managing symptoms of IBS. Meditation, including Yinnergy, can help to reduce stress, which triggers IBS symptoms. It can also help to improve gut motility and reduce inflammation. The practice of meditation can help to soothe the digestive system, making it more efficient in breaking down food and absorbing nutrients.

Biohacking

Biological hacking, also known as "biohacking," is the process of using technology to change or improve the function of the human body. The motivations for biohacking can be varied, but often it is done to improve one's health or physical abilities, or to make up for a deficiency.

Several different methods can be used for biohacking, which will depend on the desired goal. One popular method of biohacking is the use of devices to monitor and change body processes, such as heart rate, blood sugar levels, or brain activity. These devices provide feedback that can be used to alter the body's natural processes.

Another common method of biohacking is the use of drugs or supplements to improve some aspect of your physiology or cognition. This could be as simple as using caffeine to improve focus or alertness, or something more powerful like using nootropics to enhance memory and learning ability. Many drugs can be used to improve athletic performance, such as blood doping.

Brain Hacking

In its broadest sense, brain hacking is any method or technique that can be used to improve or optimize brain function. This can include things like using dietary supplements to improve cognitive function, using brain training exercises to improve memory and attention, or using techniques like meditation to reduce stress and improve focus. In recent years, the term "brain hacking" has also been used to refer to more controversial methods of manipulating brain function, such as using drugs to improve cognitive performance, or using electrical stimulation to alter mood or cognition.

Yinnergy is a form of brain hacking because it is a technology that can be used to change the brainwave patterns of a person and the way they think, feel, or behave.

The Brain's Neural Real Estate

The brain is the most complex organ in the human body, and its neural real estate is correspondingly complex. The brain is made up of billions of neurons, each with its unique structure and function. This neural real estate is responsible for the brain's ability to process and store information and control the body's movements.

The brain's neural real estate is organized into distinct regions, each of which is responsible for different functions. The largest region is the cerebrum, which controls higher-level functions such as thinking and planning. The cerebellum controls movement, and the brain stem controls basic functions such as breathing and heart rate.

The neural real estate of the brain is constantly changing in response to experience. When we learn new information or skills, our brains create new neural connections to store this information. This flexibility is what allows us to continue to learn and grow throughout our lives.

One way that Yinnergy can increase the brain's neural real estate is by increasing the number of neurons that are active at any given time. This increase in activity can lead to new connections being formed between neurons, which can ultimately lead to an increase in the brain's overall neural real estate. Additionally, Yinnergy can also increase the size and density of existing neural connections, which can also expand the brain's neural real estate.

As you meditate with Yinnergy, you are effectively helping your brain to create new neural pathways. This means that you are increasing your brain power and capacity. In addition, as you continue to use Yinnergy, you will find that your ability to focus and concentrate will improve. This is because the brain is better able to filter out distractions when it has more neural pathways. The first time you listen to Yinnergy, you may not notice any effect. However, with repeated use, Yinnergy begins to create more neural real estate within the brain, allowing it to function more efficiently and effectively.

Flow States and Being in the Zone

There is nothing quite like being in the zone. When you are in the zone, everything flows naturally and effortlessly. You are completely focused and present in the moment. It is hard to describe what being in the zone feels like, but once you have experienced it, you will know it.

The zone is a state of flow often associated with peak performance. If you are an athlete, you might experience the zone during a particularly great performance. But you do not have to be an athlete to experience the zone. Anytime you are completely focused and present in the moment, you are in the zone.

Flow states are mental states in which people experience a feeling of complete absorption and focus on what they are doing. In flow states, people feel a sense of effortless control and are completely immersed in the activity they are doing.

Flow states are associated with several benefits including improved problem-solving skills and increased creativity, productivity, and motivation. Flow states have also been linked to improved mental and physical well-being. People in a flow state are more likely to achieve their goals and perform at their best.

Flow states are not the same as being "in the zone", which is a term that is often used to describe a state of peak performance. However, flow states are different in that they are associated with a sense of complete absorption and focus on what you are doing without necessarily being in an optimal performance state heightened.

Flow states are also different from "the zone" in that they can be induced by various activities. The zone is often associated with activities that require split-second decision making such as sports or military combat. Flow states, on the other hand, can be induced by any activity that allows you to focus your attention completely on the task at hand.

Yinnergy can help produce flow states. It uses binaural beats to help the brain reach a state where it is more receptive to change. When used correctly, Yinnergy can help induce flow states.

Willpower and Self-Regulation

Yinnergy is a technology that can increase one's willpower by providing a person with a sense of calm and focus, as well as by increasing the person's ability to resist temptation.

Yinnergy synchronizes the left and right hemispheres of the brain. This synchronization weakens addictions by reducing cravings and the pleasure experienced by the addictive substance or behavior.

When the two hemispheres of the brain are working together, the individual is better able to control their impulses and thoughts. This can lead to improved decision-making and increased productivity. When using Yinnergy, users enter a meditative state more easily, and experience increased clarity of thought and greater mental discipline.

Self-regulation is the ability to control one's thoughts, and actions to achieve the desired goal. It is a critical life skill that allows people to function in society and reach their potential. Yinnergy can help increase the ability to self-regulate behavior. When used correctly, it can help individuals to better control their emotions and impulses, and to make better decisions. Yinnergy can increase levels of self-regulation in people with ADHD, OCD, and other disorders. It can also improve cognitive function and increase the ability to focus.

Daily practice with Yinnergy calms the sympathetic nervous system and stimulates the parasympathetic nervous system. The sympathetic nervous system is responsible for the fight-or-flight response, while the parasympathetic nervous system is responsible for the rest-and-digest response. When the sympathetic nervous system is activated, the body is in a state of stress and is preparing for action. This can lead to increased heart rate, blood pressure, and adrenaline. On the other hand, when the parasympathetic nervous system is activated, the body is in a state of relaxation. This can lead to decreased heart rate, blood pressure, and adrenaline.

Yinnergy can help to improve the function of the autonomic nervous system. The autonomic nervous system is the part of the nervous system that controls involuntary body functions and is responsible for regulating many of the body's automatic functions, such as heart rate, blood pressure, digestion, and respiration. By using Yinnergy, you can help to train your autonomic nervous system to function more efficiently, which can lead to improved overall health and well-being.

Meditation is also an effective way to improve heart rate variability (HRV). HRV is a measure of the variation in time between successive heartbeats, and it is an important marker of cardiovascular health. A high HRV indicates a healthy heart, while a low HRV is associated with an increased risk of heart disease. There are several ways in which meditation can improve HRV. First, meditation can help to reduce stress and anxiety, which can lead to a decrease in heart rate. Second, meditation can help to increase heart rate variability by increasing the vagal tone. The vagus nerve is responsible for slowing down the heart rate, and a higher vagal tone is associated with a higher HRV. Third, meditation can help to improve blood pressure and blood flow, which can also lead to a higher HRV.

Yinnergy and Consciousness

Slowing down binaural beats and lowering the carrier frequencies are like exploring and discovering new territory deep within the ocean that no man has ever explored. By penetrating deeper aspects of the unconscious mind, we discover deeper parts of ourselves. The lower carrier frequencies help to break through any resistance in the unconscious mind and help to access those deeper parts of the self. By going deeper, we can uncover new insights and hidden potentials that can help us transform our lives.

The Psyche and the Unconscious

As mentioned earlier, brain entrainment is a process by which the brain is exposed to certain rhythmic stimuli to synchronize its own electrical activity with that of the stimulus. This process can have a profound impact on the psyche, as it can alter brainwave patterns and lead to changes in consciousness.

Our classic version of the Yinnergy program focuses mostly on deep delta, which is a powerful frequency for releasing repressed material from the unconscious mind. By using deep delta waves with lower carrier frequencies, we can access the deepest levels of the unconscious mind and release any repressed memories or emotions. This process can be extremely therapeutic and can help us to heal from past traumas.

Transpersonal Psychology

Transpersonal psychology is a branch of psychology that studies the relationship between the individual and the Transpersonal. The Transpersonal is defined as the realm beyond the individual ego or personality. It includes aspects of the psyche such as the subconscious, the super-conscious, and the transpersonal self. Transpersonal psychology is concerned with the study of the transpersonal self and its impact on the individual ego. It is also concerned with developing methods and techniques for facilitating the transpersonal self-realization of individuals. This is where Yinnergy comes in. Our technology induces various states of meditation and altered states of consciousness, including those associated with some transpersonal psychology theories.

There is some scientific evidence to support the claims made about entrainment, but of course, more research is needed. Some transpersonal psychology theories suggest that there are benefits to be gained from states of meditation and altered states of consciousness, such as experiencing different aspects of the self, expanding one's awareness, and gaining insights into the nature of reality, and Yinnergy is one way to achieve these states.

Yinnergy is a powerful tool that can be used in conjunction with transpersonal psychology to help individuals reach higher levels of consciousness. By using Yinnergy, individuals can access deeper levels of the subconscious mind, which can lead to greater self-awareness and understanding.

The Spectrum of Consciousness

Philosopher Ken Wilber is regarded as deeply knowledgeable about states of consciousness. In his book, *The Spectrum of Consciousness*, Ken proposed that there are four major states of consciousness, each of which supports the ground-unconscious in a different way.

The first state is waking consciousness, which is associated with the ego and the left-hemisphere of the brain. This state is characterized by linear thinking, a focus on the external world, and a sense of individual separateness. The second state is dream consciousness, which is associated with the right-hemisphere of the brain. This state is characterized by non-linear thinking, a focus on the internal world, and a sense of connection with the collective unconscious. The third state is deep sleep, which is associated with the brain stem. This state is characterized by a complete lack of consciousness and is considered the ground of the unconscious. The fourth state is transcendental consciousness, also known as Turiya, which is associated with the entire brain. This state is characterized by a sense of unity with all of creation and is considered the source of all consciousness.

According to Ken, meditation has a profound impact on the spectrum of consciousness. Through meditation, we can access higher levels of consciousness that are otherwise unavailable to us. This allows us to tap into our true potential and experience a greater sense of well-being.

Yinnergy has an impact on the full spectrum of consciousness by expanding one's awareness and increasing their ability to focus and concentrate. Additionally, meditation can help to develop a deeper understanding of oneself and the world around them.

The Five Levels of the Unconscious

Ken Wilber's early work of the five levels of the unconscious posits that there are different levels of depth to the unconscious mind, and that each level can be impacted by different types of meditation.

The Yinnergy program is one type of meditation that will impact all five levels of the unconscious mind and allow you to connect with them more deeply, helping to heal traumas, bring about more profound insights and realizations, and break free from the negative patterns that have been holding us back. Yinnergy is particularly effective in helping to heal the wounds of the soul.

The Ground-Unconscious

The Ground-Unconscious is a state of awareness that is said to be the source of all other states of consciousness, a state of pure being, without any content or form. It is my understanding that Wilber believes the Ground-Unconscious is the ultimate reality, and that all other states of consciousness are simply manifestations of it.

The Archaic-Unconscious

Wilber proposes that there is an unconscious mind that is the source of our primal urges and emotions. This mind is the source of our creativity, our sexuality, and our capacity for violence, as well as the source of our capacity for love, compassion, and altruism.

The Submergent-Unconscious

The Submergent-Unconscious is a realm of consciousness that is beyond the everyday awareness of most people. It is a realm that can be accessed through meditation and other spiritual practices. The Submergent-Unconscious is a powerful source of knowledge and wisdom. It is a place where we can connect with our higher selves and tap into our true potential.

The Embedded-Unconscious

The Embedded-Unconscious is another term coined by Wilber to describe the way in which the unconscious mind operates within and affects the individual. It is said to be the source of our deepest fears, desires, and motivations, and is responsible for much of our behavior. The Embedded-Unconscious is often said to be the driving force behind our need for security, approval, and love. It is also said to be the source of our creativity, as it is where our imagination and intuition reside.

The Emergent-Unconscious

The Emergent-Unconscious is a model of the mind that posits there is a hidden level of reality and an underlying level of consciousness that is constantly emerging and evolving. This level of consciousness is not accessible to our everyday awareness, but can be accessed through altered states of consciousness, such as meditation or psychedelic experiences.

Theory Maps for the Evolutionary Mind

The Critical Brain Hypothesis

The Critical Brain Hypothesis is a theoretical framework that posits that the human brain operates at a critical state between order and chaos. This theory suggests that the human brain is poised at the edge of criticality, meaning that it is at the threshold between stability and instability. The theory argues that the brain functions best when it is in a state of criticality, where information transmission is optimized, and the brain is most efficient in processing information. This idea was first proposed by theoretical physicist Per Bak, and his colleagues, who applied the concept of criticality in physics to the study of the brain.

The critical state in the brain can be thought of as a delicate balance between excitability and stability. In this state, the brain can quickly adapt to changes in the environment and can process large amounts of information in real-time. The brain's criticality is thought to be maintained through self-organization, which occurs as a result of complex interactions between neurons and other cells in the brain.

Yinnergy and other advanced brainwave entrainment programs may play a role within the concept of criticality in the brain. Yinnergy meditation may be a catalyst for brain criticality, leading to higher stages of emotional, mental, and spiritual growth and stability. This is based on the idea that Yinnergy can help to bring the brain into a state of criticality, where it is more receptive to the stimulus of the lower carrier frequencies and is more efficient in processing the information created by the neurons when stimulated by the Yinnergy technology.

In 2003, the critical brain hypothesis found experimental support from a study by John M. Beggs and Dietmar Plenz. This study showed that the human brain operates near criticality, and that the brain's activity is characterized by self-organized criticality. This means that the brain's activity spontaneously organizes itself into critical states, where information transmission is optimized. The study also showed that the critical state in the brain is maintained through neuronal avalanches (which we will get more into), which are collective dynamics that occur between neurons in the brain.

The critical brain hypothesis is based on several key concepts such as neuronal avalanches, information transmission, critical brain states, chaos and stability, the Ising model, scale invariance, subcriticality, supercriticality, and quasicriticality.

The term "neuronal avalanches" refers to the collective dynamics that occur between neurons in the brain. It is thought that these avalanches are important in maintaining the criticality of the brain, which is a state of threshold between stability and instability. In this state, information transmission is optimized, leading to an increased ability of the brain to process and transmit information. Neuronal avalanches are thought to play a key role in the dynamic processing of information in the brain and are often used as a measure of the brain's criticality.

Low carrier frequency binaural beats, especially those embedded within our Yinnergy soundtracks are thought to have an effect on neuronal avalanches and the criticality of the brain. By producing sound waves with specific frequencies and patterns, binaural beats are thought to stimulate and modulate the brain's activity. It is hypothesized that the use of low carrier frequency binaural beats can help to bring the brain into a more optimal state of criticality, leading to improved information processing and better cognitive function. This hypothesis is based on the idea that the stimulation provided by binaural beats and monaural beats can help to optimize the balance between stability and instability in the brain, resulting in more efficient information transmission and processing.

Information transmission refers to the transfer of information between neurons in the brain. This process is fundamental to how the brain processes information and is responsible for enabling us to think, feel, perceive, and make decisions. The transfer of information is achieved through electrical and chemical signals (neurotransmitters), which are released by neurons and then bind to other neurons to trigger a response. The flow of information between neurons is dynamic, meaning it can be increased or decreased depending on a variety of factors, such as changes in the environment (this would include the external stimuli created by Yinnergy), our experiences, and our thoughts. Understanding the process of information transmission is crucial for understanding the workings of the brain.

It is possible that Yinnergy's low carrier frequency binaural beats may have an impact on information transmission in the brain by modulating the activity of neurons. Binaural beats work by presenting two slightly different frequencies to the left and right ears, which creates a perceived third frequency in the brain. This perceived frequency is thought to influence brain activity and can lead to changes in brainwave patterns. If the frequency of the binaural beat is chosen correctly, it may lead to an increased flow of information between neurons, which would in turn improve the overall functioning of the brain.

The critical brain states describe the delicate balance between stability and instability in the brain, where information transmission is optimized. The concept of criticality in the brain refers to the threshold between chaos and stability, where the brain operates in a state that is neither too ordered nor too disordered. The idea is that at this critical point, information transmission between neurons is most efficient and allows for maximum flexibility and adaptability in the brain's functioning. This is important for processes such as learning, memory formation, and decision-making. The critical brain states are thought to be essential for brain function and have been the subject of much research in recent years.

This hypothesis suggests that Yinnergy has the potential to influence the critical brain states and help to optimize information transmission.

Yinnergy works by stimulating the brain, which can help to induce a state of relaxation, focus, or meditation. By influencing the brain's state, binaural beats may help to bring the brain closer to the critical threshold, where information transmission is most efficient and flexible. This, in turn, could have a positive impact on cognitive processes that depend on information transmission.

The Ising model is a simple but powerful mathematical tool that was originally developed to describe the behavior of magnetic materials. It has since been applied to various other complex systems, including the brain. The Ising model describes the behavior of a system of interacting components, where each component can have only two states, such as "on" or "off." These components interact with one another and can change state based on their interactions. This behavior can be described using equations that capture the interactions between the components. The Ising model has been used to study the critical state in the brain, as well as other complex systems, and has provided insights into the collective behavior that arises from the interactions between components in these systems.

Low carrier frequency binaural beats embedded within Yinnergy could have an impact on the critical state of the brain, as described by the Ising model. If the critical state of the brain is altered, this could lead to changes in the interactions between neurons, resulting in changes in information transmission and overall brain function. This hypothesis could be tested by conducting studies to investigate the effects of low carrier frequency binaural beats on the critical state of the brain, using the Ising model to model the interactions between neurons in the brain. If the results of such studies were to support this hypothesis, it could suggest that low carrier frequency binaural beats have the potential to positively impact brain function.

Scale invariance is a property of complex systems where the behavior of the system is unchanged regardless of the scale of observation. This means that the same patterns of behavior can be observed at different levels of organization, from the smallest to the largest. For example, if a complex system is scale invariant, it means that the same patterns of behavior will be seen in the system whether it is observed at a microscopic or macroscopic level. This concept is important in the study of complex systems, including the brain, because it helps to explain how the brain can maintain its stability despite being composed of a large number of interacting neurons.

The effects of low carrier frequency binaural beats on the brain could be scale invariant, meaning that the same patterns of behavior and effects could be observed at different levels of organization within the brain. For example, the low carrier frequency binaural beats could have an effect on the functioning of individual neurons, as well as the overall functioning of the brain as a whole. This idea could help to explain how binaural beats could produce their effects on the brain and provide insights into how they could be used to influence and optimize brain function.

Subcriticality refers to the state where the brain is functioning below the critical threshold and information transmission is limited. In this state, the brain may not be able to process information efficiently and effectively. On the other hand, supercriticality refers to the state where the brain is functioning above the critical threshold and information transmission is excessive. This can lead to the brain becoming overwhelmed and potentially leading to negative consequences. Quasicriticality refers to the state where the brain is functioning at the critical threshold and information transmission is optimized. This state allows the brain to process information efficiently and effectively while avoiding the negative consequences of both subcriticality and supercriticality.

Binaural beats, particularly low carrier frequency binaural beats, can potentially help the brain achieve quasicriticality by providing a form of external stimulation that can regulate and optimize the flow of information in the brain. By influencing the brain waves and the electrical activity of the brain, Yinnergy may be able to help the brain achieve a state of quasicriticality, where information transmission is optimized, and the brain can function efficiently and effectively. This may be particularly useful for individuals who struggle with maintaining a state of quasicriticality, such as those with anxiety, depression, or other mental health conditions. However, research is needed to confirm the hypothesis and fully understand the potential benefits of low carrier frequency binaural beats in regulating the critical state of the brain.

The critical brain hypothesis may relate to Yinnergy in several ways. First, meditation is thought to have a calming effect on the brain, reducing stress and anxiety. This calming effect is thought to bring the brain closer to a critical state, where it is better able to process information and form new connections. Second, meditation is thought to increase the plasticity of the brain, allowing for new connections to be formed and old ones to be strengthened or weakened. This increased plasticity is thought to be a result of the brain operating near a critical state, where it is more receptive to change.

In addition, meditation is not only thought to affect the brain, but also to drive spiritual growth and transformation. This is because when the brain becomes more receptive to change, it becomes more open to new experiences and perspectives, which can lead to a kundalini awakening. This awakening is said to bring about a shift in consciousness, resulting in greater self-awareness, intuition, and a deeper connection with the divine. This increased openness can be achieved through Yinnergy, a practice that has the potential to bring the brain closer to a critical state, where it is more capable of processing information and forming new connections. This process of metanoia allows the brain to evolve and reach new levels of emotional, mental, and spiritual growth.

Although the critical brain hypothesis is still under investigation, meditation in the right conditions has the potential to bring the brain to a critical state, leading to a spiritual awakening. Even enlightenment.

Hierarchy of Needs

According to Abraham Maslow's hierarchy of needs, individuals have certain needs that must be met in order to reach their full potential. One of those is the need for self-actualization, which can be met through meditation.

Yinnergy can help individuals reach their full potential by providing them with a way to quiet their minds, connect with their inner selves, and become more self-aware.

Brainwave entrainment such as Yinnergy meditation may help individuals reach their full potential by restructuring the brain and nervous system through specific frequencies and patterns of brainwave activity that help promote growth and development. Additionally, Yinnergy may help to create an environment that is conducive to learning and development, which can lead to self-actualization.

Here are the five stages within the Maslow's hierarchy of needs model:

- **Physiological Needs:** The need for food, water, shelter, and sleep. Daily practice with Yinnergy can help to stimulate the nervous system and improve physiological functions.
- **Safety Needs:** The need for security and safety. Yinnergy can help to improve cognitive functions and reduce stress levels, which can make individuals feel safer and more secure.
- **Belongingness and Love Needs:** The need for love, friendship, and belonging. Yinnergy can help to improve communication and social skills, which can

help individuals feel more connected to others and improve their relationships.
- **Esteem Needs:** The need for self-esteem and respect. Yinnergy can help to improve self-esteem and confidence levels, which can help individuals feel more positive about themselves.
- **Self-Actualization Needs:** The need to reach one's full potential. Yinnergy can help individuals to reach their full potential by stimulating the nervous system and improving cognitive functions. This stage is important because it is when people realize their full potential and become self-fulfilled. Self-actualization is a lifelong process that can only be reached by meeting all of the other needs in the hierarchy. Once people reach this stage, they are motivated by personal growth and development rather than by external factors such as rewards or punishments.

The 10,000 Hours Theory

The 10,000-hour theory suggests that this amount of practice is necessary to become a master in one's chosen field. Based on Malcolm Gladwell's research, this idea highlights that many highly successful individuals have committed at least 10,000 hours to honing their skills. However, it is important to note that achieving expertise is not solely about the quantity of practice; the quality of practice is equally vital. Engaging in high-quality, focused, and deliberate practice is essential for attaining mastery.

As mentioned in an earlier section of this book, traditional meditation necessitates three hours of daily practice for 20.8 years to amass 50,000 hours. In contrast, Yinnergy is a program that employs binaural and monaural beats to aid individuals in meditation. Designed to enable deeper meditation, we are claiming that Yinnergy has the efficiency of multiple hours of traditional meditation within just one hour. Consequently, using Yinnergy allows practitioners to reach the equivalent of 10,000 hours in a significantly shorter time span, facilitating a faster journey to mastery of their true selves by obtaining higher-quality practice more efficiently.

It is crucial to bear in mind that other factors, including interpersonal and intrapersonal life experiences, spiritual insights, and acquired knowledge and wisdom, also play a role in becoming a true master of one's true nature. While Yinnergy serves as a valuable tool for expediting the process, it is imperative to combine it with these other components for a comprehensive mastery experience. Now, just imagine the potential for growth and self-discovery if one were to invest the actual 10,000 hours in Yinnergy practice, accelerating the mastery process even further.

Open and Closed Systems

The theory that open systems are necessary for life was first proposed by James Lovelock in the 1970s. There is an enormous amount of information regarding open and closed systems and their role in evolution, but essentially, a closed system is one where energy cannot enter or leave, while an open system is one where energy can flow in and out. In terms of evolution, a closed system would not be able to support life as new energy could not come in and support the organisms.

The human body is an open system. It exchanges energy with its surroundings through various channels, such as the brain, the nervous system, and endocrine system. When the body is stimulated by a low carrier frequency such as Yinnergy, it entrains to that frequency and exchanges energy with it. The exchange of energy between the brain and the surrounding environment is essential for its proper functioning. The brain uses the energy to maintain its structure and to carry out its functions.

Without the exchange of energy, the brain would eventually die.

Low carrier frequency brain entrainment can be seen as a stimulus that drives the flow of matter and energy within the system. In this case, the stimulus would be the low frequency carrier signal that drives the entrainment process.

The flow of matter and energy within the system is what allows for the evolution of the system. In the case of the brain and nervous system, it allows for the growth and development of nerve cells and the formation of connections between them. The low carrier frequency brain entrainment signal, such as the frequencies embedded within Yinnergy, can be seen as a catalyst for the evolution of the system by helping to create the conditions that are necessary for that system to evolve.

Chaos Theory

The Critical Brain Hypothesis, previously discussed, is closely related to Chaos Theory, which is the study of complex systems with many interconnected parts that can influence each other. Chaos Theory posits that these systems tend towards chaos, constantly changing and unpredictable. However, order can also emerge from chaos, allowing for the identification of patterns within this apparent disorder. Similarly, the Yinnergy program works to create order out of the chaos present in the mind, brain, and nervous system.

Yinnergy is among a select few brainwave technologies grounded in the understanding that chaos is a natural state from which order can arise. This concept aligns with Chaos Theory's assertion that order is an emergent property in complex systems that tend towards chaos.

During or after meditation with Yinnergy, you may experience emotional and mental turmoil, which represents a chaotic state. Although this might seem counterintuitive, it enables you to become more receptive to new ideas and thoughts. Yinnergy's chaotic state also helps you release old, restrictive thought patterns.

Utilizing Yinnergy allows you to train your brain for increased efficiency and effectiveness, ultimately resulting in a more ordered state of mind. Your brain begins to form new neural pathways, leading to enhanced mental function and a brighter outlook on life. In this sense, Yinnergy serves as a tool for transforming the chaos of the mind into order, ultimately fostering a more peaceful state of mind.

The Evolutionary Process

Yinnergy can help people to evolutionarily advance over time. By providing a way to access higher states of consciousness, Yinnergy can help people to move beyond their current limitations and reach new levels of understanding and awareness. In the past, people had to rely on trial and error to find new ways of doing things. This was a very inefficient process, and often resulted in people making the same mistakes over and over again. With Yinnergy, people can learn from their mistakes and move on to new and better ways of doing things.

Yinnergy is designed to help people evolutionarily advance. It can help people reach new levels of understanding by providing a way to access higher states of consciousness. In these higher states, people can see things from a different perspective, achieve greater insights, and enhance their creativity. This can help them to make better choices in their lives and to evolve in positive ways. With the support of other self-help practices, Yinnergy can also help people to overcome their fears and to become more confident. By facing their fears in a safe and controlled environment, people can learn to overcome them and to become more confident in their ability to handle challenging situations.

Additionally, Yinnergy can help physically change the brain in ways that support these higher states of adaptation and evolution. Thus, regular practice of this entrainment can help create an environment within the brain that is conducive to evolution and support the evolution of consciousness.

The One Hundredth Monkey Effect

The One Hundredth Monkey Effect is a phenomenon whereby a new behavior or belief spreads rapidly by contagion from one group to all members of a society, after a critical number of individuals adopt the new behavior or belief.

The One Hundredth Monkey Effect has been used to explain a wide variety of phenomena, from the sudden popularity of certain fads to the spread of political revolutions, to the popularity of the hula hoop to the fall of communism. However, there is no scientific evidence that the effect exists, and it has been criticized as a form of magical thinking.

The One Hundredth Monkey Effect is named after a purported incident that took place on the Japanese island of Koshima in the 1950s and the term was first coined by Japanese primatologist Kinji Imanishi. Imanishi, who was studying a troop of wild macaques, observed that the monkeys would wash sweet potatoes in the sea to remove the dirt before eating them. He noticed that only a few of the monkeys were doing this at first, but within a few weeks, all the monkeys in the troop were doing it. Imanishi called this the "One Hundredth Monkey Effect" and believed that it was due to the monkeys sharing their new behavior with each other until it became a tradition.

Yinnergy is an audio program that produces certain brainwave frequencies to stimulate specific changes in brain activity. The theory behind Yinnergy is that if enough people use the technology, the collective unconscious within the collective consciousness will change, and this could lead to positive changes in the world. Some people believe that the One Hundredth Monkey Effect is related to Yinnergy and other transformative programs, which can help spread new ideas, behaviors, and higher consciousness through a population.

Integral Theory

Integral Theory is a comprehensive framework for understanding reality that includes all aspects of the human experience, from the physical to the spiritual.

Ken Wilber, the originator of Integral Theory, describes it as a "theory of everything". Integral Theory provides a map of reality that includes all of the major perspectives and shows how they all fit together.

Meditation is a process of self-transformation that leads to a more integrated way of being. Integral Theory sees meditation as a key tool for personal and spiritual development. It is a means of accessing higher states of consciousness and expanding one's awareness. Meditation can help to bring about a more balanced and harmonious way of living.

The Integral Theory model of development posits that there are four main states of consciousness, each of which can be further broken down into substates. The four main states are: waking, dreaming, deep sleep, and transcendent. Each state has its own unique characteristics and functions, and are not static, but rather dynamic, giving rise to the other states (such as alertness, arousal, shock, happiness within the same waking state of consciousness).

Yinnergy, in conjunction with an integral practice, is a method that helps individuals vertically climb the ladder of psychological development, while horizontally (and ultimately) reach the highest state of consciousness, which is transcendence (Turiya, Turiyatitta). Transcendence is a state of pure awareness, where the individual is no longer identified with the thoughts and emotions that arise in the mind. Instead, the individual is able to witness the thoughts and emotions as they arise, without attachment or aversion. This state of pure awareness is the goal of Yinnergy and is the highest state of consciousness that can be attained.

Integral Theory is a comprehensive framework that provides a map of consciousness and a guide to human development. It is based on the premise that all aspects of our being—body, mind, and spirit—are interconnected and interdependent. The integral approach to meditation is based on the recognition that there are many paths to enlightenment, each of which has its own value and efficacy. The integral approach is inclusive, rather than exclusive, and emphasizes the importance of each individual's unique path.

Yinnergy is one of many powerful tools for attaining spiritual enlightenment. It is based on the principle of mind over matter, and the belief that we can tap into our innermost being to access a higher state of consciousness.

Both Yinnergy and Integral Theory have helped me to develop a deeper understanding of myself and the world around me. Integral Theory has also helped me to connect with my higher self, and to access the state of absolute pure consciousness. I highly recommend it to anyone who is seeking to experience a deeper level of spirituality.

Integral Theory posits that there are four main stages of development that individuals go through in their lifetime:

- The first stage, egocentric, is characterized by a focus on the self and on personal gain.
- The second stage, ethnocentric, is characterized by a focus on one's group or tribe.
- The third stage, world-centric, is characterized by a focus on the global community.
- The fourth stage, kosmo-centric, is characterized by a focus on the entire universe.

Yinnergy can be used as a catalyst to help individuals move from the egocentric stage to the kosmo-centric stage, and this is referred to as Growing Up. By learning and applying this model and meditating regularly, individuals can learn to let go of their egocentricity and become more aware of the interconnectedness of all beings. In doing so, they can develop a more global perspective and begin to care for the entire universe.

Yinnergy can help to evolve the ego-centric stage by providing a way to develop a more integrated sense of self, connect with a larger sense of community, develop a more holistic view of reality.

Yinnergy can help to evolve the ethnocentric stage by providing a tool for people to explore their own identity and the identities of others, understand and appreciate the differences between cultures, and develop a more global perspective.

Yinnergy can help to evolve the world-centric stage by providing people with a tool to access higher states of consciousness. By doing so, people will be able to become more aware of the interconnectedness of all things and develop a deeper sense of compassion for all beings, ultimately leading to a more peaceful and harmonious world.

Yinnergy can help to evolve the kosmo-centric stage by providing individuals with a way to connect with the greater whole, develop a deeper understanding of themselves and others, and help individuals develop a deeper connection with the world around them.

Yinnergy can also be used as a catalyst to help individuals move horizontally within states of consciousness from waking, dreaming, deep sleep, and into the transcendent, (which is divided into two parts, Turiya and Turiyatitta). Yinnergy can enhance waking state of consciousness by providing a more stable and coherent signal to the brain, which improves focus, concentration, and clarity of thought. Yinnergy can induce lucid dreaming, which is a state of consciousness in which the dreamer is aware that they are dreaming and can control the dream environment. Lucid dreaming can be a powerful tool for personal growth and self-discovery, and Yinnergy can help to facilitate this process.

Yinnergy can enhance deep sleep by providing the brain with a more stable and rhythmic environment. When the brain is able to experience a more regular and predictable environment, it can relax more deeply and enter into a state of restful and lucid sleep.

Yinnergy can help to gain access to the fourth state known as Turiya, a state of pure consciousness which is beyond the physical, mental, and emotional states, where one is aware of the absolute reality of the universe.

Yinnergy can also help to attain the fifth state known as Turiyatitta by providing a comprehensive and coherent framework within which to integrate all aspects of our experience. It can help us to see the interconnectedness of all things, and to realize the ultimate unity of all Being. By providing a clear and concise map of consciousness, it can help us to navigate our way to ever-higher levels of awareness and understanding.

The Four Quadrants Model

The Four Quadrants model is a framework proposed by Ken Wilber that suggests that all human experience can be divided into four distinct quadrants. These quadrants are the interior individual (I), the exterior collective (We), the exterior individual (It), and the interior collective (Its). Yinnergy is a technology that can help individuals and groups access higher states of consciousness, which can create a broader understanding and awareness of these four quadrants.

Yinnergy creates a bridge between the I (the mind) and the It (body, brain, nervous system), which affects the We (cultural, group, or collective) and the Its quadrants (philosophies, ethics, rules, policies, procedures, systems). Yinnergy can be seen as a tool for accessing the higher levels of consciousness in the quadrants. In the "I" quadrant, Yinnergy can be used as a tool for personal development and growth. In the "We" quadrant, the group can be influenced by the individual who has changed for the better as a result of Yinnergy or other personal development practice. In the "It" quadrant, Yinnergy restructures the brain and nervous system, which allows the "I" quadrant to fully express itself. In the "Its" quadrant, one may try to create better practices which is ideal for the collective.

The "I" Quadrant

The "I" quadrant, according to Wilber, is the world of the individual and of thoughts, feelings, and experiences. Meditation, according to Wilber, is a tool that can help us to access and explore the "I" quadrant through our innermost thoughts and feelings, and the depths of our own consciousness. Some of the benefits of using Yinnergy to explore the "I" quadrant include:

- **Increased Self-Awareness:** Yinnergy can help us to become more aware of our thoughts, feelings, and experiences. This increased awareness can lead to a greater understanding of ourselves and our place in the world.
- **Deeper Self-Exploration:** The altered states of consciousness produced by Yinnergy can provide access to previously hidden parts of our consciousness.
- **Greater Clarity:** The expanded states of consciousness can help us to see things more clearly, including our own thoughts and feelings. This can lead to greater insight and clarity about our lives.

The "It" Quadrant

The "It" quadrant is the brain, neurotransmitters, cells, molecules etc. It is nervous system itself which is evolving to higher levels of development through the use of Yinnergy and other practices. Yinnergy is also part of the "It" quadrant because it is objective of the subjective mind just like the brain and body.

The "We" Quadrant

The "We" Quadrant is the quadrant of relationships, groups, and collectives. It is the quadrant that contains all the other quadrants within it. Yinnergy is a tool that lowers the entropy of the individual, which may have an effect on the group.

The "Its" Quadrant

The "Its" quadrant relates to systems and the environment. One may use Yinnergy and have an insight which becomes a new philosophy, which is maintained through a practice or a new way of living which influences the actions and behaviors of others. If enough people practiced with Yinnergy, or with technologies like it, it could improve the environment by creating a more harmonious and balanced one.

All Four Quadrants

In a state of spiritual awakening, these quadrants are no longer seen as separate entities but as interconnected and interdependent parts of a larger whole. The individual self is not just an isolated entity but is deeply connected to the objective reality of the physical world, the collective experience, and the systems and structures that shape our reality.

Western Technology Meets Eastern Traditions

The mystical experiences induced through Yinnergy are complimentary to the experiences, realizations, and insights of all eastern practices and traditions. Just as these can help an individual to connect with the divine, Yinnergy can provide extra additional support for these practices to connect with the higher self. Both approaches can be a support to each other leading to deeper understandings of the self and the universe.

Mahayana Buddhism

Mahayana Buddhism is a form of Buddhism that emphasizes the Bodhisattva path, whereby individuals strive to become enlightened in order to help all sentient beings achieve nirvana.

Yinnergy creates various states of mind, including those associated with meditation and deep relaxation. It is very possible that using Yinnergy to produce brainwave entrainment could help individuals on the Bodhisattva path to reach a more advanced state of meditation and achieve a greater level of enlightenment.

Zen

Yinnergy is often used in conjunction with other relaxation techniques to help promote calm and focus. We believe that Yinnergy can help to induce a state of zen-like calm and clarity of mind.

Advaita Vedanta

There is no separate self or soul in Advaita Vedanta, only the one absolute reality which is Brahman/Para Brahman. This means that there is no individual consciousness that is separate from the universal consciousness.

Everything is interconnected and interdependent. The goal of Advaita Vedanta is to realize that our true nature is not the individual self, but the one absolute reality. Yinnergy creates a similar effect by synchronizing the left and right hemispheres of the brain. This eventually creates a sense of oneness and connectedness with the universe, until one realizes that they are the actual universe.

Vishishtadvaita Vedanta

Yinnergy is a tool that can be used to help bring about a more balanced state of mind, body, and spirit. It is based on the premise that everything is connected, and that by using certain frequencies, we can help to bring about harmony and balance within ourselves and with the world around us.

Vishishtadvaita Vedanta is a philosophical system that upholds the principle of non-duality, which states that there is only one reality, and that everything is connected. This principle can be applied to the use of Yinnergy, in that by using the frequencies to bring about balance within ourselves, we are also helping to bring about balance in the world around us, because from a nondual standpoint they are of the same substance.

Kashmir Shaivism

Holographic resonance is the basis of Kashmir Shaivism. This is the idea that all of reality is a single, unified field of energy and consciousness that is infinitely interconnected and holographically encoded. The Yinnergy algorithms create entrainment that is known to produce specific states of consciousness. When used with intention, Yinnergy can induce states of deep meditation, expanded awareness, and even mystical experiences, leading to the realization that we all are this unified field.

Taoism

Taoism is a philosophy that emphasizes the importance of living in harmony with the Tao, or the natural order of the universe. The Tao is seen as a unifying force that pervades all things, and Taoists believe that by aligning themselves with the Tao, they can achieve a state of harmony and balance. It is believed that the state of flow is a state of alignment with the Tao, and thus, Yinnergy can be seen as a tool to help people achieve this state.

Sikhism

Yinnergy is a technology that creates harmony between the mind, body, and spirit. It is based on the belief that all three aspects of the self are interconnected and need to be in balance in order for a person to be healthy and happy. Yinnergy helps people achieve this balance by providing them with a way to connect with their higher selves and the divine.

Sikhism is a religion that teaches that all people are equal, connected by the same soul to each other and to God who created everything, and that we must live in harmony.

Jainism

Jainism teaches that the soul is pure and perfect, and that only the body and mind are subject to change and suffering. Yinnergy could be seen as a way to help the soul remember its true nature and release the attachment to the body and mind.

Jainism teaches that all beings are equal and should be treated with compassion. Yinnergy could be seen as a way to help develop compassion for all beings, as well as a way to connect with all beings on a deeper level.

Jainism teaches that the universe is infinite and ever-changing. Yinnergy could be seen as a way to help connect with the infinite nature of the universe and to tap into its ever-changing energy.

Yinnergy and the Healing Process

The Journey to Healing

Yinnergy is a technology that creates a powerful, yet safe, audio experience that can profoundly accelerate healing and transformation. During the healing process, it is not uncommon for repressed material, emotional and mental upheaval, and catharsis to be experienced by individuals as they work through their issues. This can be a difficult and challenging process, but it is often necessary in order to achieve lasting healing. Yinnergy can help to release these negative emotions and memories, and to create a more positive outlook on life.

Repressed Material

Yinnergy can help you deal with repressed emotions and memories that you may have been avoiding, release built-up negative energy, and improve your physical and mental health. You can use this technology in combination with shadow work through a process of visualization and relaxation. By visualizing the repressed material and emotional baggage being released, we are accessing the unconscious mind to clear it.

Upheaval

The purpose of Yinnergy is to create positive change in your life by providing a high amplitude stimulus. However, this process can sometimes be difficult and cause upheaval in your life. Here are some tips on how to deal with this difficult process:

- Understand that the changes you are experiencing are positive. Yinnergy is designed to help you improve your life, so even though the changes may be difficult, they are ultimately for the better.
- Be patient. The process of retraining your brainwave patterns can take some time, so it is important to give yourself time to adjust.
- Be prepared for changes in your daily routine. Yinnergy may cause you to re-evaluate your daily routine and make changes to accommodate the new brainwave patterns.
- Seek support from friends and family.

The changes you are experiencing can be difficult to deal with alone, so it is important to seek support from loved ones.
- Remember that the changes are temporary. The brain is a flexible organ, and it will eventually adjust to the new brainwave patterns. The changes you are experiencing are only temporary and will eventually subside.

Catharsis

Yinnergy can bring about emotional and mental catharsis. This can be a very useful process for those who are seeking to heal from past traumas or to simply release emotions that are no longer serving them.

Yinnergy can help to create a space for healing and growth, and can be a very transformative experience. Yinnergy is known for being an aid in confronting the dark night of the soul. It helps to connect us with our innermost selves, and provides a space for us to explore our deepest fears and darkest emotions. The practice allows us to face our demons head-on, and to eventually release them from our lives.

Through Yinnergy meditation, we can learn to trust ourselves and our own inner strength, and to find the courage to face the challenges that life presents.

There are several potential symptoms that may occur during or after using Yinnergy, which is a tool that helps to induce emotional and mental catharsis. These symptoms may include: feeling emotionally charged or overwhelmed, feeling more sensitive to emotions, crying or sobbing, feeling a need to talk about emotionally charged topics, feeling a sense of relief or release, and feeling more peaceful or calm. It is important to note that not everyone will experience all these symptoms, and that some people may not experience any symptoms at all.

When using Yinnergy, it is possible to feel emotionally charged or overwhelmed. This is because the different levels of Yinnergy can help to release stored emotions and help the person to process them. Yinnergy creates a more sensitive state to emotions, which can help people feel more empathy and compassion. There is also anecdotal evidence to suggest that meditation can help people feel more connected to others and more in tune with their own emotions.

Some people who use Yinnergy report feeling emotions such as sadness or crying. I have gone through this myself. These emotions are usually a result of releasing old traumas or patterns of thinking and behaving that no longer serve the individual.

It is important to understand that Yinnergy is a tool, and not a panacea. It is not a magic bullet that will solve all your problems, or make you feel instantly better. In fact, some people report feeling worse when they first start using Yinnergy because it is designed to help you access and release repressed emotions and memories.

As you begin to release these emotions, you may feel sad, anxious, or even angry. This is normal and is a sign that Yinnergy is working. If you feel like crying or sobbing, it is okay to do so. This is a release of emotions that have been bottled up inside of you for a long time. Allow yourself to feel whatever emotions come up, and trust that Yinnergy will help you to release them in a healthy manner.

The Need to Talk

The Yinnergy technology is an immersive sound experience. When you listen to Yinnergy, you feel as if you are inside the audio, with the sounds wrapping around you. As said earlier, this effect is created by playing two different tones in each ear, which causes your brain to create a third tone. This third tone can have a profound effect on your mood and emotions. When you listen to Yinnergy, your brainwaves begin to match the low carrier frequency of the binaural beat, which can lead to a state of deep relaxation. This state of relaxation can help to release emotional and mental blocks, and it can also help to increase creativity and clarity of thought.

Many of our participants who use Yinnergy report feeling a need to talk about emotionally charged topics. This is because this technology can help to create a safe space for exploring difficult emotions. When you are in a state of deep relaxation, it can be easier to access buried emotions and to explore them without judgment. This can lead to a greater understanding of yourself and your emotions, and it can also help to foster greater communication with others.

The Self

Yinnergy has a profound effect on the id, ego, and super ego. By its very nature, the entrainment produced by Yinnergy trains the individual to focus on the present moment, which can be a challenge for the ego. The ego is constantly looking to the past or future, but meditation brings the focus back to the here and now. This can be a very powerful experience for the ego, as it allows the person to see that the past and future are not as important as they may seem. The super ego is also affected by this form of meditation, as it is forced to take a back seat to the ego. In a way, the meditative state created by the entrainment is a very liberating experience and allows the person to see that the ego is not as important as the super ego, and to let go of the need to control everything.

The Id

The "id" embodies the fundamental, instinctual aspect of our personality, driven by the pleasure principle. Present from birth, the id governs our basic needs and desires. In earlier sections of this book, we discussed the Archaic-Unconscious and the Embedded-Unconscious, which are closely related to the concept of the id. The Archaic-Unconscious, as described by Wilber, is the source of our primal urges, emotions, creativity, sexuality, and capacity for both violence and love, compassion, and altruism.

The Embedded-Unconscious, on the other hand, delves into the unconscious mind's operation within, and its influence on the individual. It is responsible for our deepest fears, desires, motivations, and much of our behavior. This unconscious aspect drives our need for security, approval, and love, while also being the source of our creativity, imagination, and intuition.

Meditation, as discussed earlier, can help manage the id by quieting the mind and allowing greater focus on the present moment. Although meditation may bring buried emotions and thoughts to the surface, it can be instrumental in handling the id. With a quiet mind, it becomes easier to observe thoughts and emotions without becoming entangled in them, which helps prevent impulsive reactions based on the id. Instead, individuals can choose to respond more deliberately and mindfully.

Moreover, Yinnergy can enhance self-awareness, which is beneficial for managing the id by enabling individuals to see their thoughts and emotions more transparently. With increased self-awareness, individuals can make better choices in responding to their impulses. In summary, Yinnergy can be a valuable tool for managing the id, as it quiets the mind, improves self-awareness, and prevents impulsive reactions.

The Ego

The ego is the individual's self-consciousness or sense of self, comprising both the conscious and the unconscious mind. It is the part of the mind that experiences and perceives the world, and it is the center of a person's thoughts, emotions, and memories. The ego is constantly changing and evolving as we experience new things and learn new information.

Yinnergy has a profound impact on the ego. In fact, the very purpose of meditation is to help us transcend its limitations. The ego is the part of us that is identified with our thoughts and emotions. It is the part of us that feels separate from others and the world around us. The ego is what we think of as our "self."

The ego is also afraid of change. It wants us to stay the same because it knows that change can be painful. Change means stepping out of our comfort zone and into the unknown. This ego is also afraid of death. It knows that death is the ultimate change and it will lead to its dissolution.

Meditation practices such as Yinnergy help us see through the illusion of the ego. These meditative states help us to realize that we are not our thoughts and emotions. We are not our bodies. We are not our possessions. This meditation shows us that we are something much more than what the ego presents itself to be.

Ego is also the part of the self that is concerned with our image, our identity, and how we are perceived by others. It is the part of us that is worried about being liked, about being successful, and about being happy. Ego is not necessarily a bad thing. In fact, ego can be helpful. It can motivate us to do things that we might not otherwise do. It can help us to feel good about ourselves. However, ego can also be a hindrance. When we are too focused on ourselves, we can miss out on what is happening around us. We can become self-centered and insensitive to the needs of others. We can become so wrapped up in our ego that we forget to live.

Meditation allows us to step out of our egos and to see the world from a different perspective.

We become less focused on ourselves and more on the world around us. Yinnergy can help us to connect with our true nature, which is beyond the ego. When we connect with our true nature, aspects of the ego will start to fall away naturally.

As we go through each level of Yinnergy, it is natural for us to try to distract ourselves from any discomfort that may come up. We may do things like oversleeping, overeating, watching too much television, or engaging in sex. These are all ways that we try to avoid confronting any issues that may be causing us discomfort.

However, it is important to recognize these distractions for what they are. They are simply a defense mechanism that our ego uses to protect itself from discomfort. If we can recognize them and make note of them, we can then begin to work through them.

It is important to remember that we all experience these distractions at times. They are a natural part of the human experience. What matters is how we deal with them. If we can recognize them and work through them, we will be better off for it.

One way to deal with these distractions is to become the witness with full awareness. This means that we watch what comes up without bias or resistance. We simply observe and take note of what is happening. This can be a helpful way to start working through the discomfort that may come up while listening to Yinnergy.

Another way to deal with these distractions is to work with them directly through psychotherapy sessions and shadow work. This means that we confront the issues that are causing us discomfort head-on. By becoming the witness, we can begin to detach ourselves from our thoughts and emotions and see them for what they are. This is the first step to constructively dealing with them.

The Super Ego

The super ego is a term used by Ken Wilber to describe the part of the psyche that is responsible for our sense of morality and conscience. It is the part of us that tells us what is right and wrong, and that punishes us when we do something wrong. The super ego is important for our social and moral development, but it can also be a source of conflict and anxiety.

Yinnergy can have a huge impact on the super ego. Through meditation, we can develop a deeper understanding and awareness of our super ego, which can lead to a more harmonious relationship with it. When we are more in tune with our super ego, we can better manage its demands and expectations, and find a more balanced and healthy way of living.

Anima and Aminus

In his book, *Sex, Ecology, Spirituality*, Ken Wilber introduces the idea of the Anima and Aminus. The Anima is the feminine principle within each of us, while the Aminus is the masculine principle. Together, they are the energies that create and sustain life. Wilber believes that we all have both Anima and Aminus energy within us, and that we need to balance these energies to be healthy and whole.

Meditation such as Yinnergy can help balance the anima and aminus psyche of the mind by providing a space for introspection and self-reflection, allowing us to become more aware of the underlying causes of our thoughts and behaviors, and helping us to make more positive choices in our lives.

As mentioned earlier, shadow work is another powerful tool that can help to improve the anima and aminus psyche of the mind. This process involves facing our fears and traumas, and working through them so that we can heal and move on. This can be a difficult and challenging process, but it can ultimately lead to a more balanced and healthy state of mind.

The Evolution and Adaptation of the Self

The mind is constantly evolving and adapting to the ever-changing environment. From the standpoint of transpersonal psychology, the mind is not only a product of our individual experiences, but also of the collective unconscious. This means that we are all connected on a deeper level, and that our individual minds are constantly influenced by the collective. As we go through life, we are constantly faced with new challenges and opportunities that require us to adapt and evolve our mind in order to meet these. Our hope is that Yinnergy becomes the catalyst that provides us with a foundation and framework of how the mind evolves and adapts.

The Environment

Our environments shape us and our experiences. Our brains are constantly growing and adapting to our surroundings, and what we see, hear, and feel affects how our brains develop. For example, when we learn a new skill, our brains create new neural pathways to store this information. Similarly, our environment can influence our mood, behavior, and thoughts. This is evident in the way that children raised in different cultures develop differently. It is also seen in how people who have experienced trauma often struggle with mental health issues later in life. Our environment can have a powerful influence on us, and it is important to be aware of this when considering our own development and well-being.

Low Entropy

Entropy is the measure of disorder within a system. In other words, the higher the entropy, the more disordered the system. Yinnergy can help to lower entropy within the subtle bodies of the individual, and when the individual is able to let go of thoughts and worries, they are able to reach a state of calm, allowing the neurological system to adapt and evolve. By slowing down the brainwaves and by lowering the carrier frequencies, this state of calm becomes apparent.

Yinnergy is an effective way to lower entropy by helping the individual focus on the present moment, making them less likely to worry about the past or the future. This allows the individual to let go of entropy-producing thoughts and worries. By listening to the embedded frequencies within our soundtracks, the individual can reach a state of inner peace and harmony.

With Yinnergy, the practitioner enters a state of deep relaxation in order to allow the body to release all excess energy. This process of release lowers entropy within the individual, as it allows the body to return to its natural state.

Regarding low entropy, there is a story of the Israelites in the land of Canaan marching and playing music around the walls of Jericho. This is a story that has been told for centuries.

The story goes that the Israelites were instructed by God to march around the walls of Jericho for seven days. On the seventh day, they were to march around the walls seven times, and then they were to blow their trumpets. As they blew their trumpets, the walls of Jericho came tumbling down.

This story is significant because it shows how marching in formation and blowing their trumpets on cue is an example of low entropy and high amplitude, and any system that creates such entropy can also impact the brain and nervous system. When the Israelites were marching and playing music around the walls of Jericho, they produced the entrainment that had a physical effect on external structures, a phenomenon today heavily researched by scientists. This story is a perfect example of how low entropy can have an impact on people, places, and things. Though they were at war, and many lives were lost, this metaphor demonstrates the potential of brain entrainment, and how it can help us evolve and grow as individuals.

Conclusion

The Yinnergy program can help you improve your life in many ways. It can help you increase your intelligence, focus, and concentration, as well as reduce stress, anxiety, and depression.

Yinnergy is also a great way to improve your overall health and well-being on all levels. It is safe, effective, and easy to use Yinnergy is ideal for spiritual growth and transformation. It is a powerful method that can help you to connect with your higher self, and to become more attuned to your spiritual needs. At the level of the psyche, this program can help you to release old patterns and beliefs that no longer serve you, and to embrace new ways of being that are more in alignment with your true nature.

Overall, Yinnergy is an excellent tool for anyone who is seeking to deepen their spiritual connection and to create lasting change in their lives.

I would like to say from the bottom of my heart, thank you for reading all about the Yinnergy program and all its amazing benefits. This program has truly helped me improve my life in so many ways, and I know it can do the same for you. I hope you take the time to try it out for yourself and see how it can change your life for the better. I hope that you have found this book helpful and that you will consider trying our program for yourself. It really is life-changing! Thank you again for reading.

Appendix

Yinnergy audio soundtracks can help you meditate easily and effectively. In traditional practices, it can take a considerable amount of time to perfect the art of meditation. However, with Yinnergy, you can achieve a meditative state with very little effort. All you need to do is sit in a comfortable chair and close your eyes. You do not need to clear your mind, say a mantra, or even focus on a candle flame. Though it still takes discipline to remain seated with your eyes closed, it is much easier than traditional methods.

How Does Yinnergy Work?

Yinnergy Purge, which is the pre-level, begins with Track 1, titled "Beginning". This track consists of audio tones that guide you from a high alpha brainwave state down to a very low delta/epsilon brainwave state. The soundtrack then moves on to Track 2, titled "Completion." During this track, your low delta/epsilon brainwave state is maintained to allow for stimulation to the brain/nervous system. This is when the system develops most readily.

What is on the Yinnergy Soundtracks?

We use a precise mathematical sequence of beat frequencies arranged in a careful configuration. Meditators will hear natural sounds like a babbling brook or rushing waves of water in the background, as well as the technology itself. Each meditative soundtrack consists of 12 layers, each made up of different beat frequencies and low carrier frequencies. These 12 layers work together to create a code that allows the human brain to reach a state of sound perfection. This exposes the bio-mechanism to subtle energies created by the mathematical equations. The frequencies contained within the soundtracks are highly effective in developing the brain and nervous system, though they are not easily discernible by the human ear.

How Long Does It Take to Complete the Pre-Level of Yinnergy?

The average person requires a minimum of 16 weeks to complete Yinnergy Purge, but it may take up to 24 weeks in total.

What Are People Saying About Yinnergy?

The feedback from Yinnergy meditators is exceptional. Meditators report the following results after long-term use with Yinnergy:

- Euphoric feelings and a sense of calm
- Heightened relaxation and a general sense of ease
- Stronger intuition and increased creativity
- Heightened awareness and sharpened focus
- Increased level of intelligence

Yinnergy meditators often report feeling euphoric, calm, and relaxed after using the program for a long period of time. They also say they have increased creativity, focus, and awareness. Some people say they have even had mystical experiences while meditating or dreaming.

Do You Have to Be an Experienced Meditator to Use Yinnergy?

Yinnergy is a great tool for anyone who wants to improve their meditation practice. It is perfect for beginners and experienced meditators alike. If you are an experienced meditator, Yinnergy will help you to deepen your meditation and accelerate your spiritual growth.

Some benefits of using Yinnergy every day include:

- Experiencing profound deep meditation
- Reducing stress levels and anxiety
- Having an enhanced immune system
- Feeling more happiness with a smoother flow in your life
- Emotional, mental, and spiritual growth
- Deeper levels of relaxation
- Increased feelings of vitality and rejuvenation
- Increased self-awareness
- Increased empathy and compassion
- Increased learning abilities
- Enhanced creativity and problem-solving abilities
- Increased motivation and confidence
- Greater intuition
- Improved focus and concentration
- Stimulating the creation of new neural pathways and whole-brain functioning

Yinnergy helps you access your abundant inner resources by encouraging the development and evolution of your brain and nervous system. This allows you to tap into higher states of consciousness and well-being, giving you the ability to overcome challenges and achieve your goals.

The purpose of Yinnergy is to help you connect with your highest consciousness and explore your infinite potential. The program acts as your guide as you delve into your own consciousness. Over time, Yinnergy helps you release dysfunctional feelings and behaviors. This program and other similar programs give insight to your True Nature and your higher self.

People who practice Yinnergy are often striving to bring their whole brain and subtle bodies (also known as the "aura") into a state of harmony. Yinnergy develops and enhances your conscious state, your observing state, and your awareness mind, fusing these into one.

Yinnergy meditators have consistently gained the benefits of this highly effective program because of its facilitation of whole brain thinking. In conventional meditation methods, when the meditator focuses on a word, a mantra, a koan (a story, dialogue, question, or statement which is used in Zen practice), or a candle flame, the two hemispheres of the brain start to synchronize with one another, a process known as whole brain thinking, or whole brain functioning. Only approximately 1% of our world's population can use the brain at this level on a regular basis. This makes meditation a fundamental component of self-actualization and peak performance. A more balanced brain leads to peace of mind, deeper awareness, more compassion, higher intelligence, and heightened creativity.

Instructions for Yinnergy Purge

Use Yinnergy Purge Pre-Level Beginning and Completion (available for download at https://true2soul.com/yinnergy).

- For the first 14 days, only listen to the first 30 minutes, but you can choose to go through the full hour.
- After the 14 days, listen to the full hour every single day for 4 to 6 months. Always listen to the first 30 minutes (Beginning), as well as the second half (Completion). Always listen to soundtrack with stereo headphones, sitting up, or lying down with eyes closed. To receive the full benefit of this technology, you will need to use stereo headphones. Any quality of headphones or earbuds will work, but headphones provide the best sound quality.
- After around 2 or 3 months of listening, you can choose to listen for another hour.
- **Caution: Do not overuse the soundtracks.** Please wait 2 or 3 months before

increasing your practice to 2 hours or wait until you are no longer pushed by the stimuli. Overuse of the soundtrack may result in overstimulation of the nervous system, which may lead to extreme catharsis. Yinnergy is a very powerful tool and is the equivalent of multiple sessions of traditional meditation.
- Also, if you feel emotionally, mentally, or physically overwhelmed by the actual stimuli (which may show up within a few weeks), you can cut your meditation to half an hour or you can choose to stop your practice for a couple of days, then pick up where you left off.

Vortex-Based Mathematics Bonus Chapter

In the context of the Symbol of Enlightenment, a 9-point circle developed by Marko Rodin, the numbers 1 2 4 8 7 5 (which add up to 27, and when the digits of that sum are added together equal 9) are of particular importance. These numbers are part of a complex mathematical sequence that also includes the remaining numbers 3 6 9 (which add up to 18, and when the digits of that sum are added together equal 9). This group of numbers is known as the "family group," and is comprised of the odd and even numbers of the family groups 147 and 285. These numbers function within their own algorithm, known as the 6 9 3 3 9 6 sequence. The Symbol of Enlightenment and the significance of these numbers is believed to hold the key to unlocking greater understanding and enlightenment.

When these nine numbers are arranged in a circle, 9 is the highest number. Anything over 9 becomes 1 again, with 1 representing the quantitative aspect of the number 10 (1+0=10) and so on. The numbers 1 2 4 8 7 5 are used in various ways, such as forming a 3D skin of a torus (a donut-shaped object), creating doubling circuits, nexus keys, and X, Y, and Z axis, as well as nested vortices and equipotential major grooves. These numbers are the qualitative of quantitative numbers and are used in a process known as number crunching or digital root, which was introduced to the West by the Greek philosopher and mathematician Pythagoras.

Polarity

Everything in nature exhibits polarities, with certain elements or qualities having opposite or reverse counterparts. This concept can also be applied to the numbers 1, 2, 4, 8, 7, 5, which are considered to be moving forward, and the numbers 5, 7, 8, 4, 2, 1, which are considered to be moving in reverse. When the top numbers are added to the bottom numbers, (1+5 = 6, 2+7 = 9, 4+8 =12/1+2 = 3, 8+4 = 12/1+2 = 3, 7+2 = 9, 5+1= 6) the resulting single-digit numbers are 6, 9, 3, 3, 9, and 6 (6+9+3+3+9+6 = 36, 3+6 = 9).

These single-digit numbers can represent any multiple-digit numbers, such as whole numbers like 10, 29, 37, 100, or decimal numbers like 1.0, 2.9, 3.7, 0.1, etc. In Vortex- Based Mathematics, the middle numbers are obtained by adding the top and bottom numbers, but for the purpose of brainwave entrainment, a different approach is taken. By subtracting the carrier frequency from its onset frequency, the difference between the two is obtained, giving us the beat frequency. This beat frequency is responsible for inducing a state of entrainment in the individual listening to Yinnergy, which can mimic the effects of meditation.

To determine the proper onset and base frequencies for a given application, we can use the numbers 1, 2, 4, 8, 7, and 5 as a guide. For example, if we want to use the digital root numbers 1 (onset) and 5 (base), it is important that the quantitative value of the root number 1 is greater than its base, which is 5. To find the beat frequency in this case, we can simply subtract the base frequency from the onset frequency, like so: 1 over 5 becomes 10 minus 5, which is 5; 2 over 7 becomes 11 minus 7, which is 4; 4 over 8 becomes 13 minus 8, which is 5; 8 minus 4 is 4; 7 minus 2 is 5; and finally, 5 minus 1 is 4. This gives us the beat frequencies 5, 4, 5, 4, 5, 4 (5+4+5+4+5+4 = 27, 2+7 = 9). It is important to note that in the context of sound, all these numbers must remain the same, with the quantity able to be raised or lowered, but the quality must not be changed. The special relationship between these numbers in the correct order forms the basis of this technology. To illustrate this concept with an example, if we have an onset frequency of 211.4 Hz (2+1+1+4 = 8), then the base frequency could be 211 Hz (2+1+1 = 4) or any other number that can be reduced to 4, as long as it is lower than the onset frequency.

The Physics Behind Low Carrier Frequencies

Left ear frequency (f_L) = 223.1 Hz - 17.1 Hz = 206.0 Hz

Right ear frequency (f_R) = 211.0 Hz - 17.1 Hz = 193.9 Hz

In this equation, the left ear plays the onset frequency, which is a tone that changes over time. The right ear plays the carrier frequency, which remains constant throughout the duration of the binaural beat session. The beat frequency is subtracted from both the onset and the base frequencies, producing the same beat frequency, but a new lower carrier frequency which becomes the deeper level with a higher amplitude.

Within all levels of the Yinnergy program, the binaural beat frequency is the perceived difference between the onset frequency and the carrier frequency, as perceived by the brain. In this case, the binaural beat frequency ranges from 12.1 Hz to 3.1 Hz as the onset frequency changes and the carrier frequency is applied.

Here is another example: If we take a tone of 211.4 Hz, which is the onset frequency, and subtract it by 17.1 Hz, the new resulting frequency will be 194.3 Hz. When this number is reduced to a single digit, it remains an 8, as the digits of the frequency sum to 8, and the digital root (or the single-digit result obtained by adding all the digits together) is also 8. Similarly, if we take the new onset frequency 194.3 Hz and subtract it by 17.1 Hz, the resulting onset frequency will be 177.2 Hz, which also has a digital root of 8. The same is true for the carrier frequency, but in this case, the set of numbers is reduced to a 4. This demonstrates how the digital root of a number can provide important information about its underlying qualities and characteristics, and can be a useful tool when applying Vortex-Based Mathematics to brainwave entrainment.

In summary, Yinnergy levels are created using a combination of brainwave entrainment and Vortex-Based Mathematics, utilizing principles such as polarities and the special sequence of numbers known as the Symbol of Enlightenment. The use of these techniques allows for the creation of sub-binaural rhythms, which can affect the complexity and activity of the human brain. However, the effectiveness and validity of these concepts in influencing brain activity or consciousness is currently a matter of debate and further research is needed to fully understand their potential effects.

The Importance of Sound Physics in Brainwave Entrainment

Sound physics plays a crucial role in the effectiveness of brainwave entrainment techniques, such as binaural beats. The principles of sound physics, including frequency, wavelength, and the speed of sound, are all essential factors that determine the ability of a sound to affect the brain and induce changes in brainwave patterns.

Frequency is a measure of the number of oscillations or vibrations of a sound wave per second, and it is measured in hertz (Hz). Different frequencies correspond to different brainwave patterns, and the use of specific frequencies can help to induce changes in those patterns.

Wavelength is the distance between two adjacent points on a sound wave that are in phase with each other. The wavelength of a sound wave is inversely proportional to its frequency, meaning that higher frequencies have shorter wavelengths and lower frequencies have longer wavelengths.

The speed of sound is the distance that a sound wave travels per unit of time, and it is affected by the density and elasticity of the medium through which it is traveling. In the case of brainwave entrainment, the medium is typically air, and the speed of sound is approximately 343 meters per second.

By understanding these principles of sound physics, it is possible to design brainwave entrainment techniques that are more effective at inducing changes in brainwave patterns and achieving the desired effects.

Sound physics is a crucial aspect of brainwave entrainment, and a thorough understanding of these principles is essential for the design and implementation of effective techniques.

An Example of the Yinnergy Mathematical Equations

$(f1 - f2 = 12.1)$ and $(12.1 = 1+2+1 = 4)$ and $(f1 - f3 = 9)$ and $(f3 - f2 = 3.1)$ and $(3.1 = 3 + 1 = 4)$ $(f4 - f5 = 12.2)$ and $(12.2 = 1+2+2 = 5)$ and $(f4 - f6 = 9)$ and $(f6 - f5 = 3.2)$ and $(3.2 = 3 + 2 = 5)$ $(f7 - f8 = 12.1)$ and $(12.1 = 1+2+1 = 4)$ and $(f7 - f9 = 9)$ and $(f9 - f8 = 3.1)$ and $(3.1 = 3 + 1 = 4)$ $(f10 - f11 = 12.2)$ and $(12.2 = 1+2+2 = 5)$ and $(f10 - f12 = 9)$ and $(f12 - f11 = 3.2)$ and $(3.2 = 3 + 2 = 5)$ $(f13 - f14 = 12.1)$ and $(12.1 = 1+2+1 = 4)$ and $(f13 - f15 = 9)$ and $(f15 - f14 = 3.1)$ and $(3.1 = 3 + 1 = 4)$ $(f16 - f17 = 12.2)$ and $(12.2 = 1+2+2 = 5)$ and $(f16 - f18 = 9)$ and $(f18 - f17 = 3.2)$ and $(3.2 = 3 + 2 = 5)$

$f1 = 223.1$ Hz (onset frequency), $f2 = 211.0$ Hz (base frequency), $f3 = 214.1$ Hz (onset frequency), $f4 = 223.0$ Hz (onset frequency), $f5 = 210.8$ Hz (base frequency), $f6$

$= 214.0$ Hz (onset frequency), $f7$
$= 222.8$ Hz (onset frequency), $f8$
$= 210.7$ Hz (base frequency), $f9 =$
213.8 Hz (onset frequency), $f10 =$
222.4 Hz (onset frequency), $f11 =$
210.2 Hz (base frequency), $f12 =$
213.4 Hz (onset frequency), $f13 =$
222.5 Hz (onset fr frequency eq),
$f14 = 210.4$ Hz (base frequency),
$f15 = 213.5$ Hz (onset frequency),
$f16 = 222.7$ Hz (onset frequency),
$f17 = 210.5$ Hz (base frequency),
$f18 = 213.7$ Hz (onset frequency).

Here we are demonstrating 12 different channels, each with a unique binaural beat frequency. We will explore each of these 12 channels in detail.

Channels 1/7: The first and seventh channels of Yinnergy utilizes a binaural beat frequency of 4 Hz. This frequency is achieved by playing a base frequency of 211.0 Hz in one ear and an onset frequency of 223.1 Hz in the other ear. The difference between these two frequencies, 12.1 Hz, is equal to 1+2+1, which reduces to 4. This channel takes 20 minutes to reach its full effect, as the onset frequency is gradually reduced by 9 Hz over this time period. The final binaural beat frequency for this channel is 3.1 Hz, which reduces to its digital root which is 4.

Channels 2/8: The second and eighth channels utilizes a binaural beat frequency of 5 Hz. This frequency is achieved by playing a base frequency of 210.8 Hz in one ear and an onset frequency of 223.0 Hz in the other ear. The difference between these two frequencies, 12.2 Hz, is equal to 1+2+2, which reduces to 5. This channel takes 20 minutes to reach its full effect, as the onset frequency is gradually reduced by 9 Hz over this time period. The final binaural beat frequency for this channel is 3.2 Hz, which reduces to its digital root which is 5.

Channels 3/9: The third and ninth channels utilizes a binaural beat frequency of 4 Hz. This frequency is achieved by playing a base frequency of 210.7 Hz in one ear and an onset frequency of 222.8 Hz in the other ear. The difference between these two frequencies, 12.1 Hz, is equal to 1+2+1, which reduces to 4. This channel takes 20 minutes to reach its full effect, as the onset frequency is gradually reduced by 9 Hz over this time period. The final binaural beat frequency for this channel is 3.1 Hz, which reduces to its digital root which is 4.

Channels 4/10: The fourth and tenth channels utilizes a binaural beat frequency of 5 Hz. This frequency is achieved by playing a base frequency of 210.2 Hz in one ear and an onset frequency of 222.4 Hz in the other ear. The difference between these two frequencies, 12.2 Hz, is equal to 1+2+2, which reduces to 5. This channel takes 20 minutes to reach its full effect, as the onset frequency is gradually reduced by 9 Hz over this time period. The final binaural beat frequency for this channel is 3.2 Hz, which reduces to its digital root which is 5.

Channels 5/11: The fifth and eleventh channels utilizes a binaural beat frequency of 4 Hz. This frequency is achieved by playing a base frequency of 210.4 Hz in one ear and an onset frequency of 222.5 Hz in the other ear. The difference between these two frequencies, 12.1 Hz, is equal to 1+2+1, which reduces to 4. This channel takes 20 minutes to reach its full effect, as the onset frequency is gradually reduced by 9 Hz over this time period. The final binaural beat frequency for this channel is 3.1 Hz, which reduces to its digital root which is 4.

Channels 6/12: The sixth and twelfth channels utilizes a binaural beat frequency of 5 Hz. This frequency is achieved by playing a base frequency of 210.5 Hz in one ear and an onset frequency of 222.7 Hz in the other ear. The difference between these two frequencies, 12.2 Hz, is equal to 1+2+2, which reduces to 5. This channel takes 20 minutes to reach its full effect, as the onset frequency is gradually reduced by 9 Hz over this time period. The final binaural beat frequency for this channel is 3.2 Hz, which reduces to its digital root which is 5.

Panning

One unique aspect of Yinnergy is that certain tones are panned to the left and right at different percentages. In this section, we will focus on the tones that are panned 100% to the left and right.

Panning, in sound engineering, refers to the distribution of a sound signal, or a specific frequency within a sound signal, across the stereo field. In other words, it refers to where the sound is perceived to be coming from in relation to the left and right headphones or speakers. When a sound is panned fully to the left, it is perceived to be coming exclusively from the left speaker. When a sound is panned fully to the right, it is perceived to be coming exclusively from the right speaker. When a sound is panned to the center, it is perceived to be coming equally from both the left and right speakers, which makes this monaural.

Panning, or the placement of specific sounds in different locations within the stereo field, is an essential aspect of binaural soundtracks. By carefully controlling the panning of different tones, it is possible to create the illusion of sound coming from specific locations in the listener's environment. This can be especially effective in inducing a state of equanimity, as it can help to create a sense of spatial awareness and immersion. The panning of specific tones is also what creates the binaural beat needed to produce the frequency-following response, a phenomenon in which the brain adjusts its own frequency patterns to match those of an external stimulus. This can be used to manipulate brainwave activity and induce states of relaxation or concentration, depending on the desired outcome. Overall, the careful use of panning is a powerful tool for creating immersive and effective binaural sound experiences.

In Yinnergy, certain tones are panned 100% to the left and right to create a specific binaural beat frequency. For example, if a tone of 223.1 Hz is panned fully to the left ear, and a tone of 211.0 Hz is panned fully to the right ear, the brain will perceive a binaural beat frequency of 12.1 Hz (1+2+1 = 4). This binaural beat frequency is thought to correspond to a specific brainwave state, such as alpha or theta, which is associated with relaxation and meditation.

By using panning to distribute specific tones to the left and right ears, Yinnergy creates a unique binaural soundtrack that can help to induce relaxation and promote brainwave entrainment. The use of panning in Yinnergy is an important aspect of the soundtrack's effectiveness and helps to create a sense of spatial awareness and immersion for the listener. For example, frequency 1 at 223.1 Hz is panned 100% to the left, and frequency 2 at 211.0 Hz is panned 100% to the right.

In Yinnergy, tones are panned not only 100% to the left and right but also at varying percentages such as 90%, 70%, 60%, 40%, and 30%. By adjusting the panning percentages, beats are created along both the binaural and monaural beat spectrum. As the panning percentage decreases, the beats shift from being predominantly binaural to more monaural in nature. For instance, when a tone of 223.1 Hz is panned 90% to the left ear and a tone of 211.0 Hz is panned 90% to the right ear, the brain perceives a binaural beat with reduced intensity but at the same frequency of 12.1 Hz (1+2+1 = 4). In addition to using different panning percentages, Yinnergy also incorporates tones that are 45, 90, and 180 degrees out of phase. This means that the waves of the two tones are not in sync with each other and are instead offset by a specific degree.

The use of out-of-phase tones in Yinnergy creates a unique sound that can be effective in promoting brainwave entrainment. The specific brainwave states associated with these out-of-phase tones will depend on the degree of offset and the frequencies of the tones being used.

By using a combination of panning percentages and out-of-phase tones, Yinnergy creates a rich and varied soundscape that can effectively induce states within meditation and promote entrainment.

While the information provided above gives a brief overview of the principles and concepts behind Yinnergy and Vortex-Based Mathematics, there is much more to this technology that cannot be fully conveyed in this book. It is important to note that this is just a small sample of the many complex and fascinating facets of this technology and much more lies beneath the surface. While it may be tempting to delve deeper and uncover all the secrets behind Yinnergy and Vortex- Based Mathematics, it is ultimately up to the individual to explore and discover the full extent of this technology and its potential applications.

As I said earlier, the technology behind Yinnergy is based on the principle that everything in the universe is living numbers manifested by the number nine. The theory states that when we align our ourselves with that of the universe, we can tap into an infinite supply of this number which is of mathematical perfection. The number nine is the number of completion and represents the highest level of consciousness and beyond.

The Vortex- Based Mathematical algorithm of the numbers 1, 2, 4, 8, 7, 5 is, in my opinion, the neurological equivalent of feng shui. Just as it is believed that feng shui can create a sense of balance and harmony in your home, the Vortex-Based Mathematical algorithm can create a sense of balance and harmony in your mind. Just as the placement of furniture and other objects in a room can impact the flow of energy, so too can the neural structure of your brain and the release of neurotransmitters impact the flow of energy in the body.

The Yinnergy meditation technology is also based on the Vortex-Based Mathematical algorithm of the 1, 2, 4, 8, 7, 5, governed by the sacred numbers of the 3, 6 and 9 which is the mathematical equivalent of the Ming-era design of the taijitu (the yin and yang symbol). The 6 (2+8+5 = 15, and 1+5 = 6) being the yin, the 3 (7+1+4 = 12, and 1+2 = 3) being the yang, and the 9 (1+2+4+8+7+5 = 27, and 2+7 = 9) being the S curve in the middle of the symbol. This technology can be used to help people achieve a state of inner peace, balance, and even enlightenment.

About the Author

After a spiritual awakening in 2008, Morgan O. Smith devoted his life to helping others find inner peace. He is a teacher of nonduality, certified meditation instructor, and brainwave entrainment facilitator. He is also the founder of mind@ease in schools for the Toronto District School Board; a youth outreach worker currently under the ministry of Children, Community and Social Services; and a former facilitator for the Strengthening Families Program (SFP). He has received several awards for his commitment and dedication for his work and community at large. Morgan created Yinnergy

Meditation, a grassroots project that encourages emotional, mental, and spiritual growth through audio-induced deep meditation, and the Yinnergy Appreciation Awards in 2011 to acknowledge youth who have made a positive impact on the community. His mystical insights have also inspired the thought provoking, and critically acclaimed book, The God Behind The God, written by Arian Herbert in 2015.

Morgan is a philanthropist who donates his time and resources to many other projects. He has contributed financially to non-profit organizations, grassroots community initiatives, radio projects and documentaries, such as The Shift, The Connected Universe with Nassim Haramein, and Morgan's Kids. He appeared on a public service announcement for Boost Child Abuse Prevention and Intervention in 2013, and appeared in the video *Beloved Flowers* by Ontario's first Poet Laureate, Randell Adjei & Aaron Ridge in 2021. He also participates in scientific studies for institutions, such as the Institute of Noetic Sciences (IONS).

Morgan was a Gemini Award-winning comedy writer, stand-up comedian, and television personality before seeking a more spiritual path. He has shared the stage with comedy greats such as Kevin Hart, Dave Chappelle, Patton Oswalt, and the late Robert Schimmel and was voted one of Canada's top three favorite comics by the Gemini Awards

People's Choice Award in 2003. Over his career, Morgan has appeared in almost fifty television shows, indie films, and documentaries, and was featured in five mixtapes for Canadian independent hip hop artists. Most notably, he was a co-host of the Award-winning television show *Buzz*. The show earned a cult following during its nine seasons for its guerilla-style approach and off-color humor.

Manufactured by Amazon.ca
Bolton, ON